YouTube PAYCHECK

YouTube PAYCHECK

by Corey Flecken

Notifuro Publishing

tta! Your Soul — Anime Reviews & Japan

YouTube
PAYCHECK

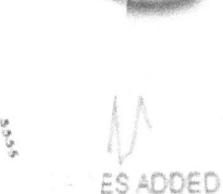

ARN OVER $25K A YEAR MAKING VIDEOS

"It sounds like you have a really great channel brewing, can't wait to see it!"

-RPM Network

"Congratulations! You've been selected to access the Maker Studios Talent Dashboard."

-Maker Studios

"It would be great if we could discuss partnering your channel further with you! "

-The Gamer Nation (TGN)

"I watched the episode of HaraHetta you submitted and absolutely love it."

-Blip TV

Copyright © 2013
Corey Flecken

All rights reserved.
No part of this publication may be reproduced, stored in a retrieval system or transmitted in any form or by any means electronic, mechanical, photocopying, recording or otherwise, without the prior written permission of the author.

Trademarks
YouTube, Google, the YouTube logo, the Google logo, YouTube.com, Google.com, and related trade dress are trademarks or registered trademarks of Google Inc,. and/or its affiliates in the United States and other countries and may not be used without written permission. All other trademarks are the property of their respective owners..

Published by
Notifuro Publishing
www.notifuro.com

Edited by
Stephanie Sztan

Illustrations, layout and design
Corey Flecken
www.coreyflecken.com

ISBN: 978-0-578-12575-6
Printed in the United States of America

about the author

Hajimemashite! I am Corey, for the last two years I have been working on a successful YouTube show which has been generating close to $2,000 to $3,000 per month
どうぞよろしくお願いします

In 2011 I went to Japan to study the Japanese language. I went right after the tsunami and radiation alerts. Everyone I knew told me not to go because they feared for my life. Going to Japan was a life long dream for me and I simply replied, "I would rather die trying to achieve my goals rather than hiding from them."

YouTube earnings are a great source of extra income. Below is a snapshot of what you can earn by making videos on YouTube. **Roughly $2,109.14**

about the author

When I first started making money like everyone else, I splurged. I got a Honda S2000 and did some body work to the car. I was still working a full time job and living at home but making extra cash on the side. No one truly believed that I could be making money via YouTube but I proved them wrong.

about the author

After spending two weeks in Spain visiting my cousin (who is a child music star and actor for Disney Spain) *seen below with the dreadlocks*. I realized having a nice car and money is not what is important. The Spanish drive around in beat up cards just to get to work. Nothing more nothing less. When I returned from Spain I sold my S2000 to start my goal on going to Japan.

about the author

While I was in Japan going to school in Osaka. I started to film more footage for my show. This is when it started to really take off. I was bridging a certain gap to the American audience from Japan. Sadly, I removed most of my original videos due to copyright rules which I didn't know when first starting my show. Recently YouTube deducts any removed or private video views from your channel which negated a large sum from my statistics but still remains under 'lifetime' views internally.

about the author

Between affiliate marketing, my YouTube show and part time contract work, I am able to lead a very relaxing life and travel when I want to. The reason I wanted to write this book is because EVERYONE I have told that I am making money off YouTube did not believe me. They think it is impossible. Well it is not impossible, I think people who are making money with YouTube are trying to keep it a secret. Just like anything else in this world, if you have inside information on when to buy and sell stock, would you tell someone? People are greedy and want to keep that strategy to themselves. You only live once and another dream of mine is to become a motivational speaker and help others be successful and happy with their lives. I have talked to many American celebrities about their problems via Skype to the point I have to go invisible not to be bothered. I am also working on a clothing line with actor Cary-Hiroyuki Tagawa called 'Notifuro' which should be a lot of fun.

table of contents

hapter   *Page*

1. What is your show about? 19
   (finding a niche, research competition, etc.)
2. Organizing Data 22
   (email, social media, dot com/tv, video sites, etc.)
3. Preparing to film 30
   (camera, lighting, background, audio equipment, etc.)
4. Filming & Editing 40
   (video software, audio software, screen capture, etc.)
5. Posting Videos 46
   (promote your videos, description, keywords, etc.)
6. Channel Tweaking 56
   (editing the way your channel looks)
7. Start Making Money 71
   (join google adsense, become a youtube partner, etc.)
8. Tracking Analytics 83
   (see how popular your show is, views, likes, subscribers, etc.)
9. Join a YouTube Network 97
   (how to apply to networks and make more money)
10. Only Foresee Success 108
    (my thoughts on what your end goals should be)

bonus chapters

A. **Video Game Recording**
   (how to record while playing your PC video games)

B. **How to Live Stream**
   (setting up your computer to stream yourself or shows)

C. **Custom YouTube Video Buttons**
   (ever wonder how some videos have really cool buttons in their videos, learn how here)

D. **YouTube Ad Information**
   (more details about the types of ads YouTube & networks use)

E. **Monetized Video Still Under Review**
   (YouTube has a bug where you can not gain money until your videos pass review! I walk you threw a trick that works for me about 85% of the time.)

F. **Fighting Copyright Strikes**
   (don't fret over copyright strikes, fight back!)

before we begin

Creating a YouTube show is an amazing experience. Not only is it exciting, but once you start to earn money and create a fan base you will see that your hard work and dedication has paid off. Do not quit your day job just yet! It took me a little over a year to develop a perfect strategy and rhythm for my show. You will learn how hard it can be to film in front of a camera but amazingly fun at the same time.

I wish you the best of luck on this new and exciting adventure and I am glad that I am helping you turn your dream into reality.

joining youtube

This chapter is very basic. If you already have a YouTube account and channel name you can most likely skip to the next topic.

To create a YouTube account you will also need to create a Google account since Google owns YouTube. I suggest creating the Google account first because it is an easier process this way. Go ahead and go to: http://www.google.com

In the top right you will notice a red 'sign in' button. Click on the button and it will bring you to a login in page. In the same area where the sign in button was it should now say 'sign up', click here again. You will be brought to the create a new account with Google page. Enter your information into the corresponding fields. Note that your mobile number should be active because Google might send a text message to verify your account once complete.

joining youtube

Verify your account

Enter verification code

Didn't get your code? Sometimes it can take up to 15 minutes. If it's been longer than that, try again.

After you verify your account, Google will ask you how you would like to appear within Google+. If this account will be used primarily for your YouTube show, you should update it to match your show's name. For example, one of my channels name is RuggedSource therefore I would make the first name 'Rugged' and last name 'Source'. You can always change this later so do not worry if you make a mistake. There should be a 'next' button on the page followed by a blue 'Get started' button.

Welcome Corey!

Now you're ready to search, create, and share across all of Google products. Check out your new account in the upper right corner. From there you can update account settings, and view account settings for kids, families. You'll also soon find tips on what to do to get most from all of Google.

Your new email address is cookingwithcoreyf@gmail.com

Thanks for creating an account. Have fun!

Get started

joining youtube

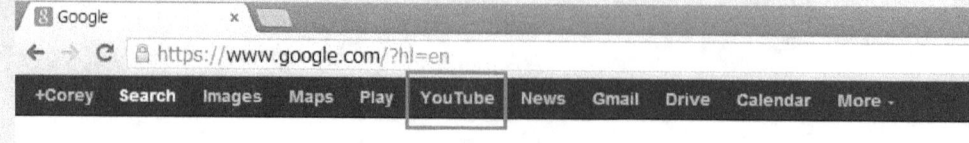

We will continue to create our YouTube account or in better terms 'link' the YouTube account to your Google account. At the top of Google's site you should see a YouTube button, click on that. It will bring you to YouTube. You should still be signed into Google but when you are at YouTube's site, it will have a blue 'sign in' button in the top right. Click the button and it will ask you to re-log into Google. Now in the top right of YouTube you should see your name and icon, etc. Click on the small grey arrow next to your icon to expand the Google options. Then click on the 'My Channel' url.

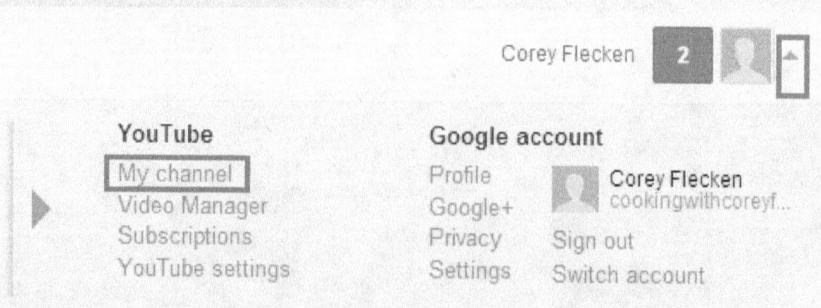

joining youtube

By default Google will ask you if you want to use YouTube as your Google+ details. DO NOT click OK. Click on the blue text which says 'To use a business or other name, click here."

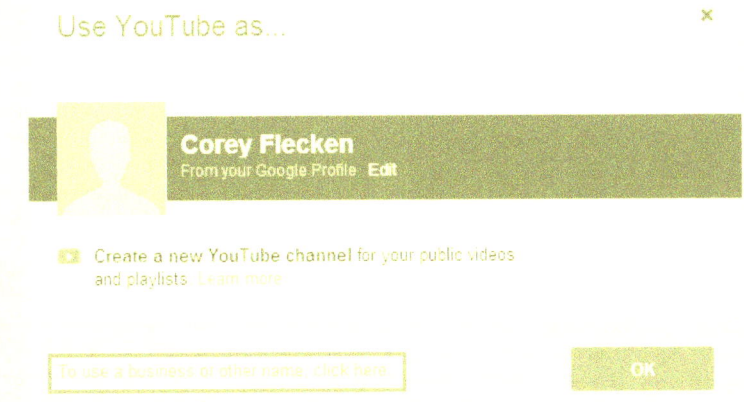

The next window will ask you to name your YouTube account. You cannot use spaces or other characters in your name. So make sure you are happy with your name before you continue. Once your name is available and you are satisfied, click the 'OK I'm Ready' button.

joining youtube

Create your YouTube channel

Creating a YouTube channel lets you upload videos, create playlists and respond to videos with comments. Learn more

Upload videos
Videos you upload to YouTube will appear on your channel if you make them public.

Create playlists
With a channel you'll also be able to create playlists. If you make a playlist public it will be associated with your profile.

Comment
Your comments and likes will be associated with your profile. You can control if they appear on your channel by adjusting the sharing settings here.

Want to use your Google Profile information on your channel? Create a profile channel

How you'll appear on YouTube
Username: Check availability

CookingWithCorey

Your username can contain only letters and numbers
Username available!

OK, I'm ready to continue

Don't worry about the look and feel of your YouTube landing page now. I will explain in later chapters how to edit and update your profile to benefit you the most. I could suggest making your channel private until you are ready to start posting videos. To do this, in the top right of your account name, click on the grey arrow and go into the 'settings' options. Under account information there is a URL for 'Advanced'. In here you can either delete your channel or make it private. Click on the 'make private' button.

Account Information

Name

CookingWithCorey
cookingwithcoreyf@gmail.com
Link channel with Google+
Advanced

Change

what is your show about?

Before starting a YouTube show, you need to figure out what you'd like your show to focus on. If you have seen one of my YouTube shows you will already know that my favorite show is about Japanese Anime and Gaming. Sometimes I also include other random videos to give viewers a sense of entering my personal life. I believe if you do this, you give your viewers an opportunity to feel connected to you on a personal level. Since YouTube becomes your point of interaction, you have to think of creative ways to build a friendship with your viewers.

what is your show about?

I would stick to a genre that you already enjoy talking about. The more you are familiar about a subject, the easier it is to speak about on camera. If you have never spoken on camera before, you will find out it is harder than you think.

Below is a few examples of YouTube shows you might want to create:

 Design/Crafts Show

 Technology Sho[w]

 Political Show

 Gaming Show

 TV Gossip Show

 Shopping Show

 Sports Show

 Etc.

what is your show about?

If you're still having difficulties discovering what kind of you show you'd like to develop, go to the homepage of YouTube (www.youtube.com) and click into one of the main categories listed on the left hand side. You will then be brought into a sub category of the more popular YouTube channels. Browse around until you have found exactly what you want to speak about.

Popular on YouTube
- Music
- Sports
- Gaming
- Movies
- TV Shows
- News
- Spotlight

organizing data

After finding your main focus point of the show, we need to create a name for the show. I usually just brainstorm name ideas because if it becomes popular it makes sense to the viewers. In the end it doesn't need to make sense. My YouTube channel is called 'RuggedSource'. That name has nothing to do with Japanese Anime & Gaming now does it? However there are some people that spend days/weeks on the name. Try to do this in a day or two. After a name for the show has been decided let's start to organize the data and details for the show.

organizing data

Open a spread sheet or notepad document. You will need to keep all details in one place. You will now need to register an email address, any social media networks and other video networks other than YouTube. Below are the steps I would take when doing this:

- Email Registration, preferably a Gmail account
- Facebook Fan Page
- Twitter
- Tumblr
- Flickr
- Instagram
- Daily Motion
- MetaCafe
- Any dot com or dot tv you wish to use
- Etc.

organizing data

Site	User	Pass	Email
gmail	rugbyweekend	i<3rugby01	rugbyweekend@gmail.com
facebook	rugbyweekend	password123	rugbyweekend@gmail.com
twitter	rugbyweekend		
tumblr			
flickr			
instagram			
dailymotion			
metacafe			
rugbyweekend.tv			

Now that your spreadsheet has all your user names and passwords in it, (http://wp.me/a3AbPD-16 to download a pre-made spreadsheet by myself for free) You will want to setup 'Google Alerts'. This will ensure that you have up to date information and news on the genre for your show. To start this go to: http://www.google.com/alerts

organizing data

What is Google Alerts?

Google alerts will email you once there is an update to a blog or website on the keyword you have set for your alert. This is important if you want to be the first to announce any news on the subject you talk about via the world of YouTube. You will earn respect on being able to produce up to date videos on the fly.

organizing data

Organizing your email with filters and labels will help with the day to day business of running a YouTube show. Depending on which email client you use this will be different but very similar. I will be using GMAIL in this example. If you are not using GMAIL then just google 'how to setup email filters with <insert mail client here>'.

When you load gmail near the left where you have your default folders, towards the bottom there will be an option called 'Create new label'. Select this option. A new window will appear asking you to name your label.

Create a label for each social media or any other site(s) you have signed up for previously.

organizing data

Also do not forget to create a label for your Google Alerts. You want to have every email coming in labeled so you understand exactly what to do when you wake up and check your mailbox.

Next, you need to set up filters for your emails so they go into the labeled folders and skip the inbox. You will want to tick an email from a certain domain. Once it is highlighted, select the 'more' option and then 'Filter messages like these'. Please follow the next set of images below to finalize the filter creation process:

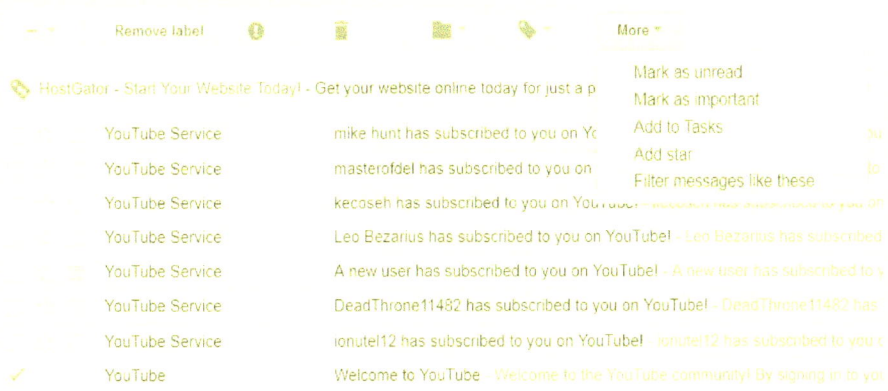

organizing data

```
from:(noreply@youtube.com)
```

Filter	✕
From	
noreply@youtube.com	
To	
Subject	
Has the words	
Doesn't have	
☐ Has attachment	
🔍	Create filter with this search »

The filter option will automatically apply to the from email. Sometimes I also like to include 'Has the words' option or Subject line. When Facebook sends you emails their subject line can be "John Doe Liked Your Page". So I will remove the from filter option and add in the subject area "Liked Your Page". Now any Facebook emails for page likes go into my filter.

organizing data

from:(noreply@youtube.com)

« back to search options

When a message arrives that matches this search:

☑ Skip the Inbox (Archive it)
☐ Mark as read
☐ Star it
☑ Apply the label: YouTube ⇵
☐ Forward it   add forwarding address
☐ Delete it
☐ Never send it to Spam
☐ Always mark it as important
☐ Never mark it as important

Create filter   ☑ Also apply filter to **8** matching conversations

Learn more

- Skipping the inbox means the email will go straight into your filtered label.
- Apply the Label: Select the corresponding folder the emails apply to.
- If you have any matching emails still in your inbox folder, the apply option will also send any of those emails to the new filter created. (I always do this)

preparing to film

Not everyone has money to spend on a studio for their show. I will discuss what I did and how much it cost to create my studio. However, creating a unique studio will make your show stand out and climb ahead of the competition.

First you need to decide what camera you will be using. I chose the Nikon D5100. I believe it was around $520 at the time I purchased it. I get all my digital and audio equipment at B&H Photo. You can visit their site here: http://www.bhphotovideo.com/

Also search for sales and wait for deals on holidays like Cyber Monday.

preparing to film

I understand that $520 is a large amount of cash to put down to start your show. Like I said earlier, I wanted to make sure I did everything correct when making my show to be better than your typical basement/room YouTube reviewer. BUT those creators are still making money, I am not knocking them. However, once you reach a certain point with your show and want to reach out to a network to make more money. Who do you think they will chose in the end? A YouTube creator with a show in their room or a show with a semi professional studio. I was just awarded a contract with TGS (the game station). They do not have any requirements in terms of monthly views, the only requirement they have is QUALITY.

preparing to film

A clear example of why it is important to do this. You can always start small then gradually increase your shows production quality. This is up to you. Below is what I purchased starting off:

- Nikon D5100 Camera
- Azden WLX-Pro Wireless Lapel Mic Set
- Halogen Stand Work Lights
- White ply board
- Custom Wallpaper

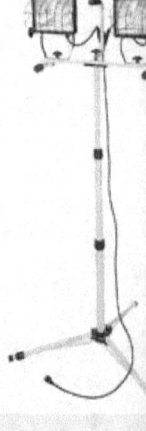

preparing to film

The camera and lavalier set I purchased from B&H Photo:
http://www.bhphotovideo.com

The halogen stand work lights and white ply board was purchased at a home improvement store such as Lowes or Home Depot. I got two 6" halogen lights, one 3" halogen light and one floor halogen light. Below is the setup I used for my studio and the lights:

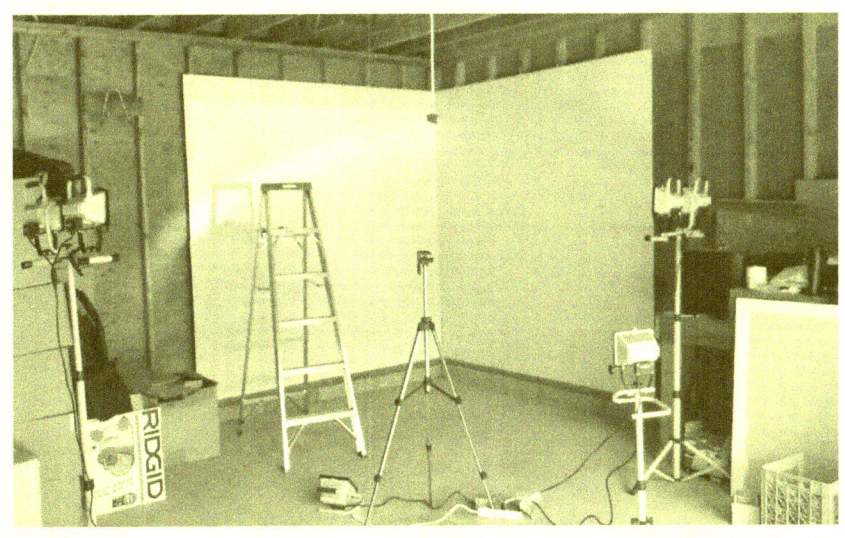

preparing to film

- Camera - $520
- Lights - $90
- Audio Equipment - $140
- Ply Board - $28
- Wallpaper - $75

Total: $853

Now after making my show and buying lights, I found this company on Amazon that has really cheap lightning equipment for $60. They are called 'Cowboy Studio', an example of their equipment is below:

preparing to film

Another route is to go the green screen method. I will be doing this shortly in my shows. You can purchase a really good green screen kit for close to $200 which includes the following:
- Three (3) High Quality Light Sockets
- Three (3) 45 Watt 5000K Compact Fluorescent Daylight Light Bulbs
- One (1) Mini Light Stand
- Two (2) White Translucent Photo Umbrellas
- Two (2) Top quality Light Stands
- One (1) Complete Background Support Set (includes tripods and cross bar)
- One (1) Carrying Case for Background Support
- One (1) Black Seamless Muslin Backdrop
- One (1) Green Seamless Muslin Backdrop
- One (1) White Seamless Muslin Backdrop

For more details on this equipment go here:
http://goo.gl/k3fGD

preparing to film

If you can not afford to do this in the beginning, another suggestion is to use a home made green screen. I made a green screen first before creating my studio. You might be able to find a cheap green screen kit but what I did was I went to an arts & crafts store, bought a huge sheet of green material for $40. Next I went to a home improvement store and while in the store I literally crafted a frame out of plumbing pipes. The frame was about 6 feet tall and 6 feet wide. I attached the green fabric to the frame and booted up my web camera. On the next page you will see how I was testing the green screen with background options for my show.

preparing to film

Lighting is very important with a green screen. Below you will see I changed the green screen to be a city in Tokyo.

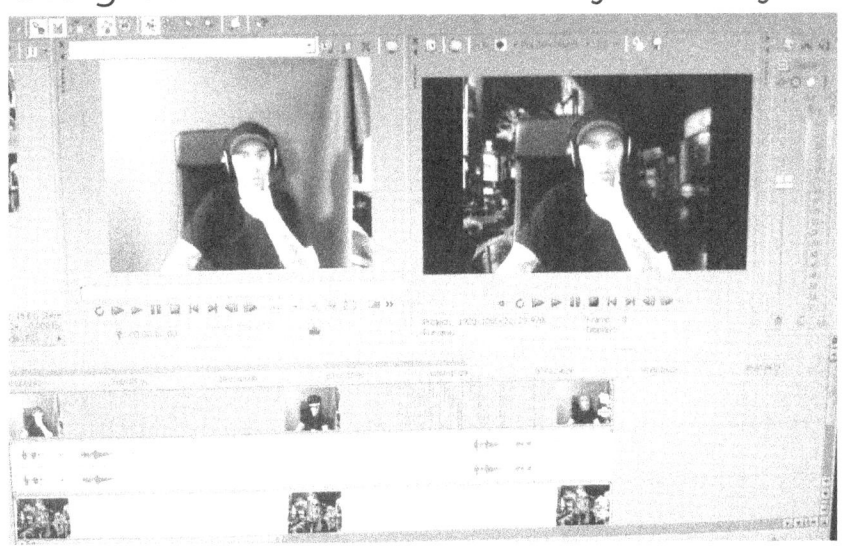

preparing to film

- Green Fabric at Joanns Crafts - $40
- Plumbing Pipe Frame - $30
- Cowboy Studio Lighting - $70

Total: $140

You do not need the Cowboy equipment, instead you can use regular lights around the house but to properly adjust the light for the green screen will be annoying every time you need to record an episode. You will need to have a perfect stretch of light on your green screen and also behind it. This is to ensure when you want to change the backdrop to something else, the color selector changes the entire green screen as expected.

preparing to film

Lastly if you cannot afford either of these options, don't worry. You can start off your YouTube show in your room or some location in your house. I would just ensure that your room is clean or has some type of memorabilia associated with your show. If your show is about comic books, I wouldn't have basketball posters in the background.

Also think outside the box and maybe once a month film your show at a Starbucks or bookstore, etc. Give the audience a sense of adventure.

filming

You will come to find filming yourself and speaking in front of a camera is a lot harder than one would think. When I first started out, my video performance was very lame and dull. I practiced every night for an hour or two on random subjects. Practice makes perfect, study other YouTube actors and how they perform. Most successful YouTube shows are properly scripted and edited like a real TV show or movie. The only difference is, the stars of the show are ordinary people that have been filming themselves for a few years now and are use to being in front of a camera.

filming

Before you start to record any take, practice what you will say. I went to Wal-Mart and bought a dry erase board to write keywords on what I would be discussing during my show. Place the board behind your camera so when you look at it, your eyes are looking into the camera and not else where.

filming

YouTube offers a website called the 'Creators Playbook': https://www.youtube.com/yt/playbook/

I highly recommend reviewing this site and read any documentation on producing an eye catching show. One of the number one laws of a YouTube show is the viewer will decide to continue to watch your show within the first 7 to 15 seconds. You will want to be able to capture the audiences attention within this timeframe.

editing

After filming your show you will need some sort of video editing software. I use a PC and the following programs:
- Sony Vegas Pro
- Techsmith Camtasia

Both programs cost a decent amount of money. They also offer trial versions which you can use for about 30 days to see if you like it enough to purchase. There are a bunch of free video editing programs which you can use. Also try to Google 'Best Free Video Editing Software' and read reviews on such programs.

YouTube also has a built in editor where you can find here:
http://www.youtube.com/editor

editing

When rendering the video try to ensure all quality is kept to HD quality. Below you will see an image of my settings in Sony Vegas. I like HD 1080 at 29.97 frames per second. Audio format at stereo mode, 48,000Hz. When exporting I use the .mp4 format with Internet HD 1080p mode.

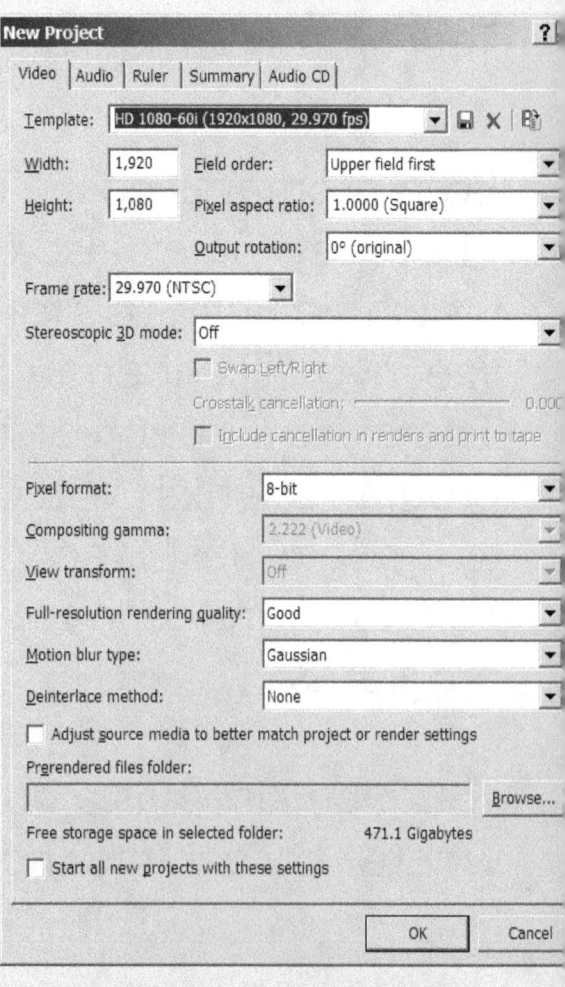

editing

If your show is based on tutorials or how-to's, you will need screen capturing software. As I stated earlier I use Camtasia Studio for this. Techsmith has a free two minute version called 'Jing' which you can use at no cost to record audio and screen movement for your tutorials. More details on Jing can be found here:
http://www.techsmith.com/jing.html

Once a week I would study how to produce different styles of footage with your software. The more creative you become with your videos, the more interesting they are to watch. The more viewers, the more income.

posting videos

When you are done editing and filming your videos, you are now ready to show them to the world. Log into your YouTube account and near the top you will see an upload option. I always like to keep my videos 'private' before making them public. Making them private you can edit the videos before anyone is able to view them. This is important because you will be adding keywords, tags, a description, annotations, etc. which will benefit your video views in the long run. You do not want a bogus video that does not funnel sales and wasted views or dropouts. You want to draw in fans and subscribers to your channel.

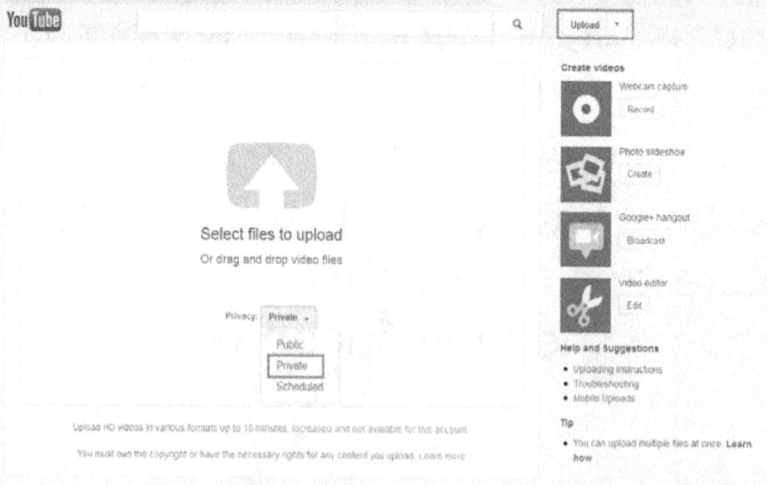

posting videos

I am very tedious and a perfectionist, after uploading my videos, I spend 3 to 4 hours tweaking all settings before pushing the videos live. Google has really good documentation which should be read during your free time. If you didn't know this by now, Google owns YouTube. Google's support page for uploading YouTube videos:
http://support.google.com/youtube/bin/topic.py?hl=en&topic=2888648&parent=16547&ctx=topic

On the next page you will see two different photos of a page after uploading a video onto YouTube. If you are just starting out, your page will most likely look like the first image. The second image is for a YouTube account which was approved to be a partner.

DO NOT upload copyrighted music or use copyrighted material in the background of your videos. Your YouTube channel will be flagged with copyright strikes and then can be eventually terminated. You cannot make money if this happens.

posting videos

Basic YouTube account view:

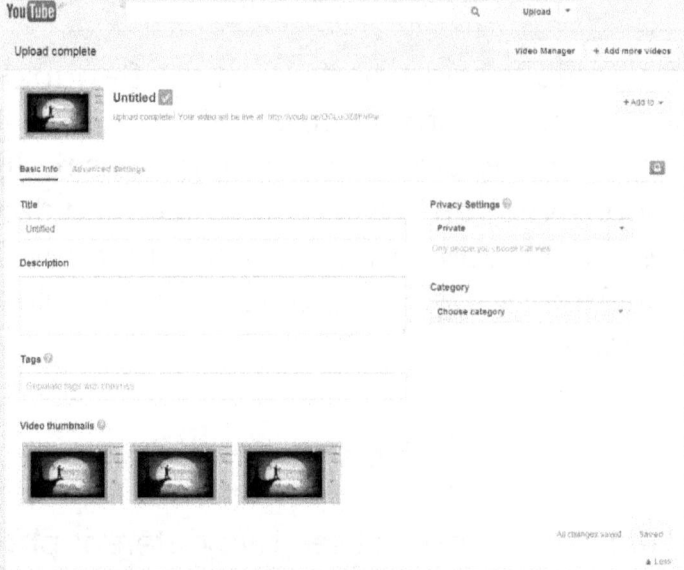

Partner YouTube account view with options highlighted:

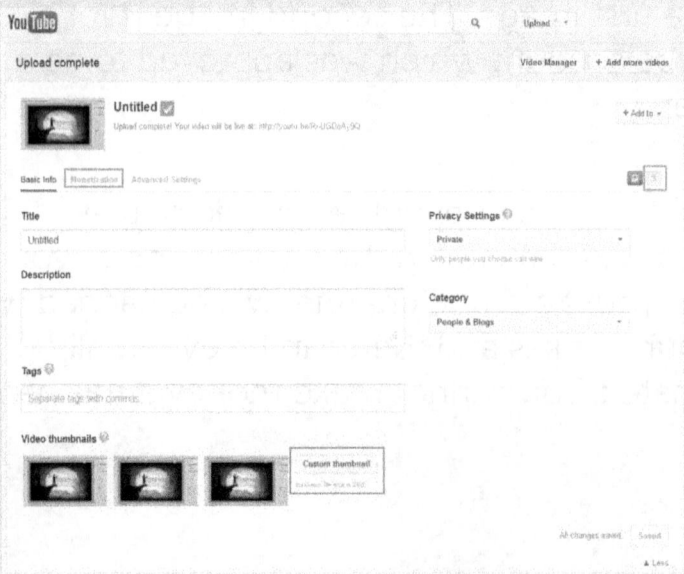

posting videos

I would like to elaborate a bit more on the copyrighted material aspect because this is something I learned the hard way. There is a document called 'Fair Use Doctrine' (http://www.copyright.gov/fls/fl102.html) which expresses how to use copyrighted material without getting in trouble. Read the above URL to fully understand what you can do. Also I have listed below what steps you should take to ensure your videos do not get flagged:

- If you are unsure, create a dummy YouTube account and upload a video there. Wait 5 minutes to see if it becomes flagged.
- Make sure you are speaking when showing footage that is not yours. Such as game play or other videos*.
- Videos* - Do not show full videos, only clips. Also try to use a pip window to show the videos. Like a news anchor show might.
- With music you are only to use royalty free music or possibly 'covered' music. With covered music all material must be original. If you steal the beat to a song and then sing over it. You are still stealing the beat. You need create everything yourself.

posting videos

After your video has been posted, don't worry about modifying the video settings right away. Make sure the video is set to 'private' & save. You can change your channel settings to allow all videos to be automatically set to private. To do this go to:

YouTube > Dashboard > Chanel Settings > Defaults

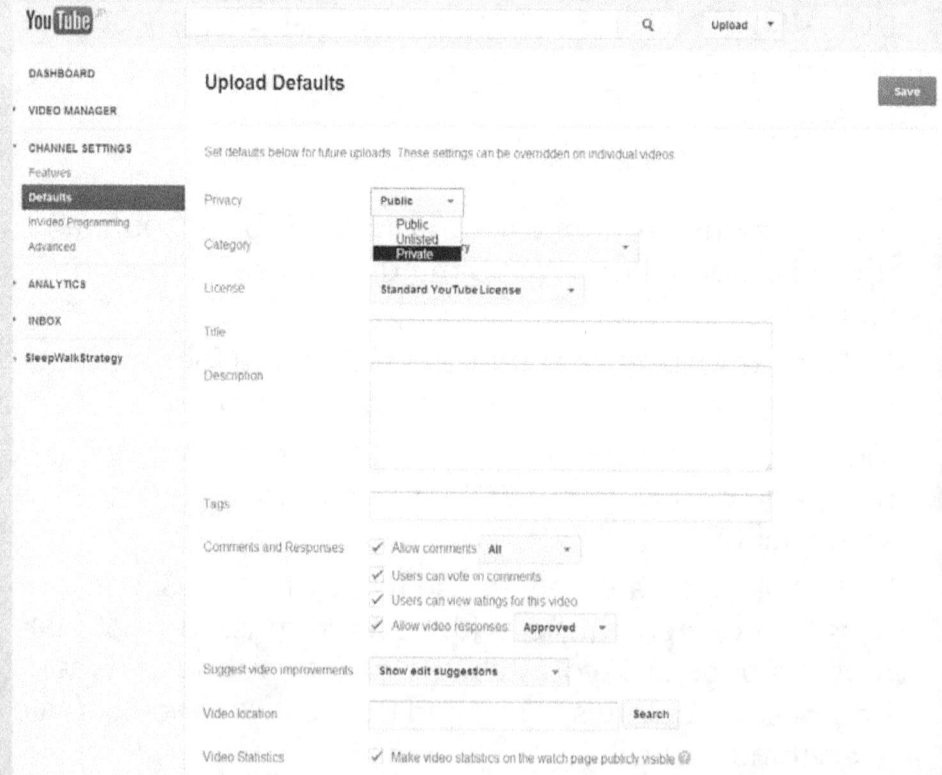

posting videos

Now we can tweak your uploads. Within the dashboard, go into the Video Manager. Here you will see all of your uploaded content. Next to the thumbnail of your videos, you will see an 'edit' button. Click on that (see below).

Title: The name of your video you posted.

Description: Explain what your video is about.

Tags: Keywords which helps YouTube determine if your video is relevant to users when searching for these keywords.

Privacy Setting: Change this to public when ready.

Category: Choose the area which best suites this video. Not your channel, but the video.

posting videos

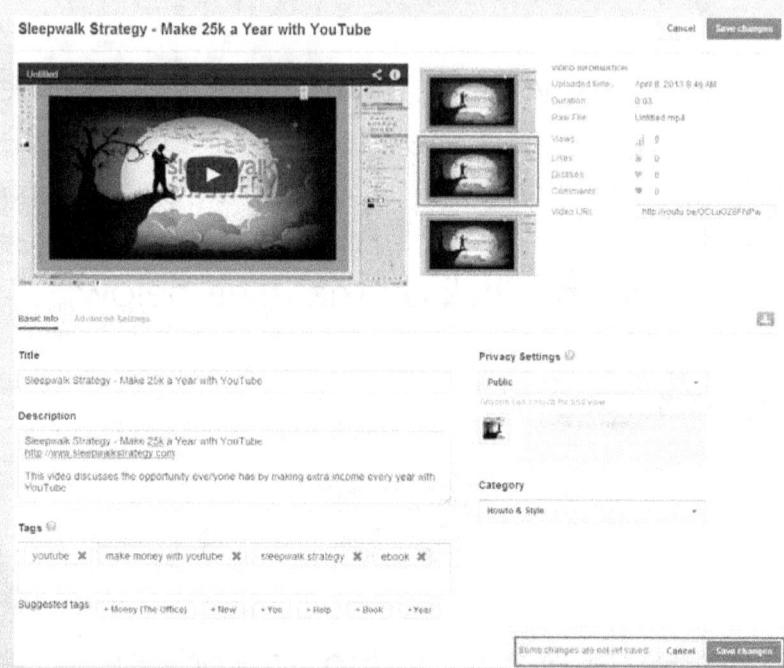

Make sure you save your changes when you are done. There have been many times I made changes then clicked into my dashboard not realizing how stupid I am. Always check the save changes notice in the bottom right to see if the video details were saved before moving elsewhere. Then click the 'Advance Settings' tab next to 'Basic Settings' under your video.

posting videos

The advanced settings are for your own personal reasons and purposes. For example, I turned off video responses. I do not want other people advertising their videos on my videos. I also removed the option to publicly display my video stats to users. Below is an example of what I use for most of my videos:

Sometimes I will make comments set to approved only. To ensure only positive feedback is left.

posting videos

Still within the video editing page, scroll up to view more options to make against your video. Click into the 'Annotations' tab.

Out of all of the settings within that row, I only use 'Annotations'. I can not express how important it is to use the annotations correctly. This is all about user engagement and promoting your other videos. Have you ever seen a video on YouTube and while you were watching you saw pop ups that said something like: 'Click Here to Subscribe', 'If you think the cat is cute click the like button', 'Comment about the prank below', etc. In all different shapes, colors and sizes? Well this is how you do it. It is time consuming and tedious but is worth doing if you want to make more money with engagement.

posting videos

Below is an example of an annotation I created using the chat bubble shape to show as if the person was talking. When a user clicks on that chat bubble, they are brought to a new page asking them to join my YouTube channels subscriber list. Your YouTube subscriber list is just like a mailing list. Every time you post a video, it is shared to all of your subscribers. The more subscribers you have the more money you will make. Yet another reason why annotations are very important to incorporate.

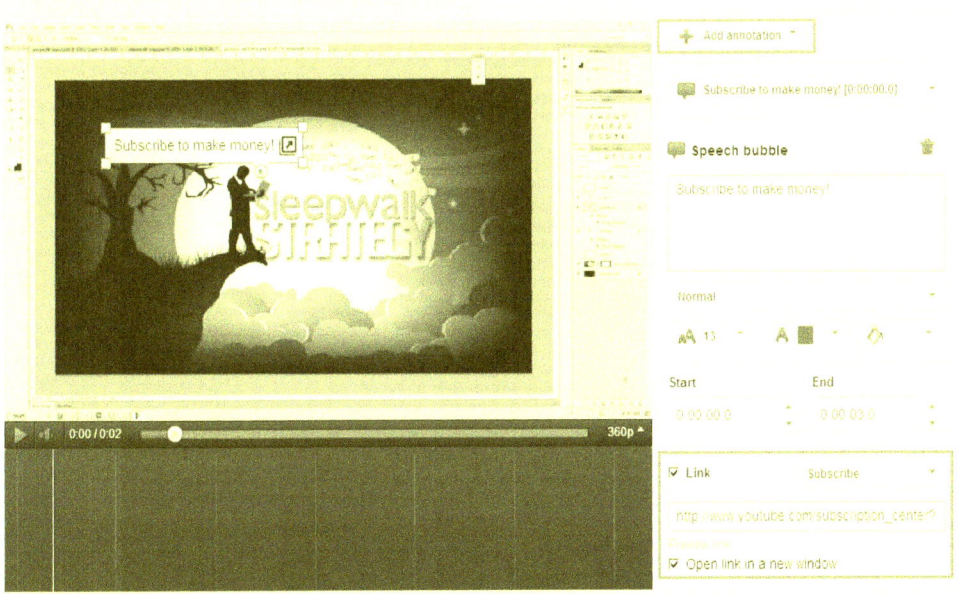

channel tweaking

With my luck, when writing this ebook, YouTube created a new layout version called 'one channel'. There is much debate on which style is better to brand your channel. To me, it really depends on your target audience. The 'one channel' layout is great for large companies and artists. The old layout I feel is better for gamers and 'how to' videos. More information on the style for your channel can be found here: https://www.youtube.com/onechannel You can revert back and forth from the old style to the 'one channel' style. All new channels created use the 'one channel' style. If you are a new user and would like to see the old version, go to the URL mentioned above and click on the link to switch back.

> You are more than the sum of your uploads. On your new channel, branding works across devices, you can reach out to non-subscribed viewers, and you can show off more of your content so fans will go deeper.
>
> (You're already using the new channels design, but can switch back to the previous design if you'd like.)

channel tweaking (old)

When logged into YouTube, in the top right you will see your user name. Click on it and in the drop down chose 'My Channel'.

You will now see your channel's home page. Select 'Channel Settings' near the top. The first tab is your channels look and feel. You can add a background image and change the background color. YouTube has a preview mode below, so when you are making changes you can see them in real time. If you do not like a change, click on the cancel button in the top right and start over.

channel tweaking (old)

The next tab is 'Info & Settings'. Here you will enter basic information on what your channel is about. If your channel is about cooking and recipes, ensure you express those details. You do not want to say you have a cooking channel, but your videos are of your cat.

- Title – A few words best describing your channel.
- Description – Detailed verbiage about your channel, videos and of yourself.
- Tags – Similar to the tags (keywords) when editing your videos. When a user is on another channel watching cooking videos, your channel might appear in the 'related channel' section.

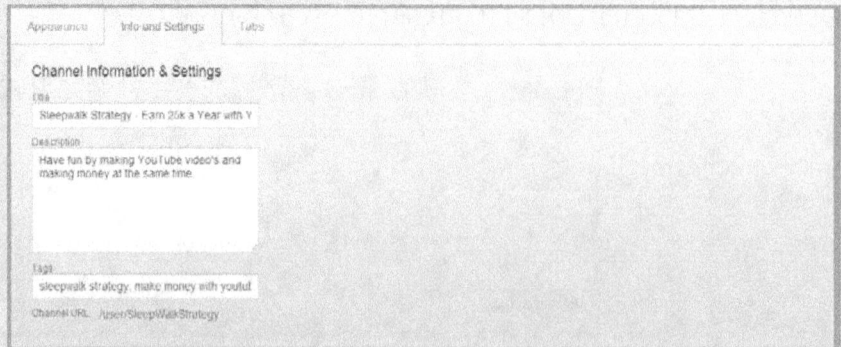

channel tweaking (old)

Lastly the 'Tabs' tab. The first option you will see a dropdown for something called 'Default Tab'. When a user lands on your channel page, they will be brought to the selected option. The 'Featured' panel gives you the ability to choose how your videos and information will be displayed. The 'Feed' panel contains personal options to display to your subscribers if you comment or like a video, etc.

Below are my usual channel settings:

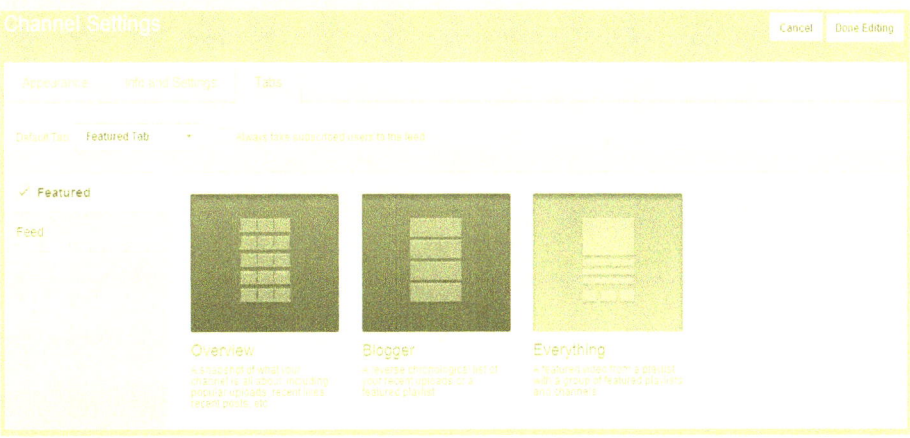

channel tweaking (old)

Depending on which featured option you have selected, you channel will have certain options to edit in different areas. Your channel should look similar to the image below:

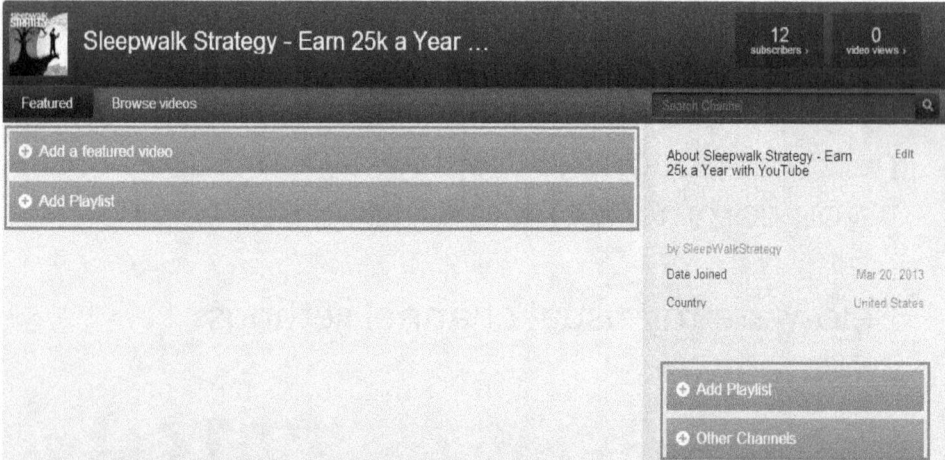

Notice the blue+ bars to tweak against your channel. You will want to edit all of these options to benefit your channel the most. To add a playlist, you need to create a playlist. I like to create playlists of my own videos rather than of other videos other users created. The more playlists you have of your videos the better.

channel tweaking (old)

Now lets get really creative and start to customize your channel to add your social media widgets and more text to be indexed by Google. You will see an 'edit' button near the top right (see above) click on this.

The first box is a text box to enter as much detailed information about your channel as possible. Next is where you enter in your social media URL's and other website details. If your website has a favicon setup, this will appear in the icon box. If not a default globe icon will appear.

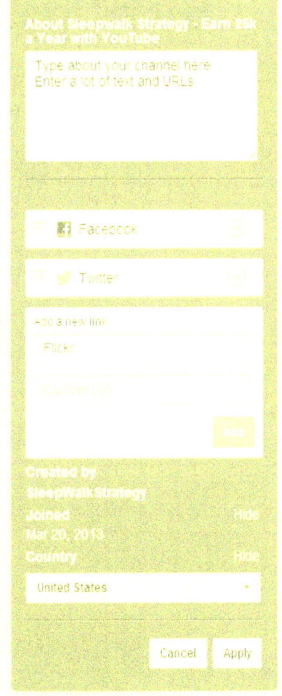

channel tweaking (old)

The last options are to show/hide when you joined YouTube and also the country your channel originates from.

If you are curious on how some channels have more options and buttons on their page, this is because they are partnered with networks. When you are partnered, you get special branding options to promote your channel better. This is your ultimate goal. Also if you are no graphic artist or do not know how to create a YouTube layout for your channel, just use Google to find a company or someone that can.

More information on channel optimization can be found here: https://www.youtube.com/yt/playbook/channel-optimization.html

channel tweaking (new)

The new layout settings allow your channel to be viewed on mobile apps and webTV's. I have been more focused on producing videos and editing content. However, we will explore the new options together. Remember the new layout is called 'one channel' and more details can be found here:
https://www.youtube.com/onechannel

Below is a screenshot where I highlighted the editable areas of onechannel. You will not see the edit buttons until you move your mouse over the areas. Also make sure you are on the 'About' tab within your channel's home page.

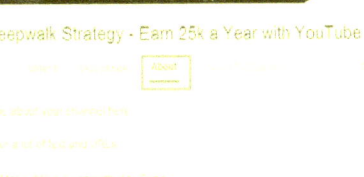

channel tweaking (new)

Let's start from the top left and go downwards. Changing the channel icon. When you hover over the small thumbnail image you can click on the edit button. This will pop up a new window asking you to upload an image. The suggested size is 800px x 800px but less than 1mb. You can also use a scene from one of your videos which you have uploaded.

Your thumbnail icon will be what associates your YouTube page when leaving comments on other videos. Choose or create a good image so that users will be curious and click into your profile.

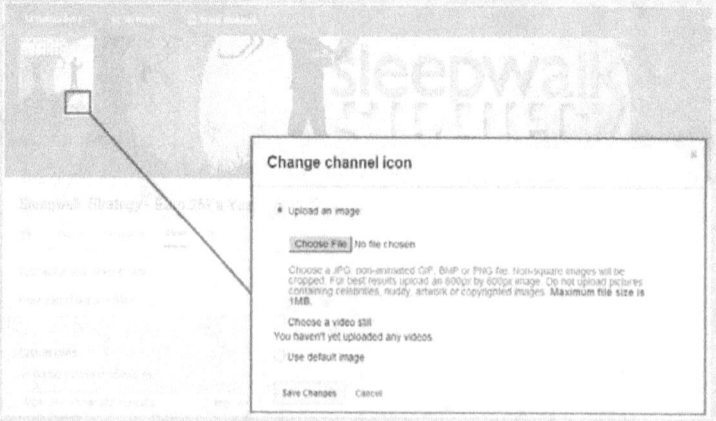

channel tweaking (new)

Across the top to the right you will be able to edit either 'links' or 'channel art'. Select the channel art option. This will load a large window. Upload a photo from your computer here to be part of your background. I highlighted the URL below in this window to help you create the image or click here: http://support.google.com/youtube/bin/answer.py?hl=en&topic=16630&ctx=topic&answer=2972003

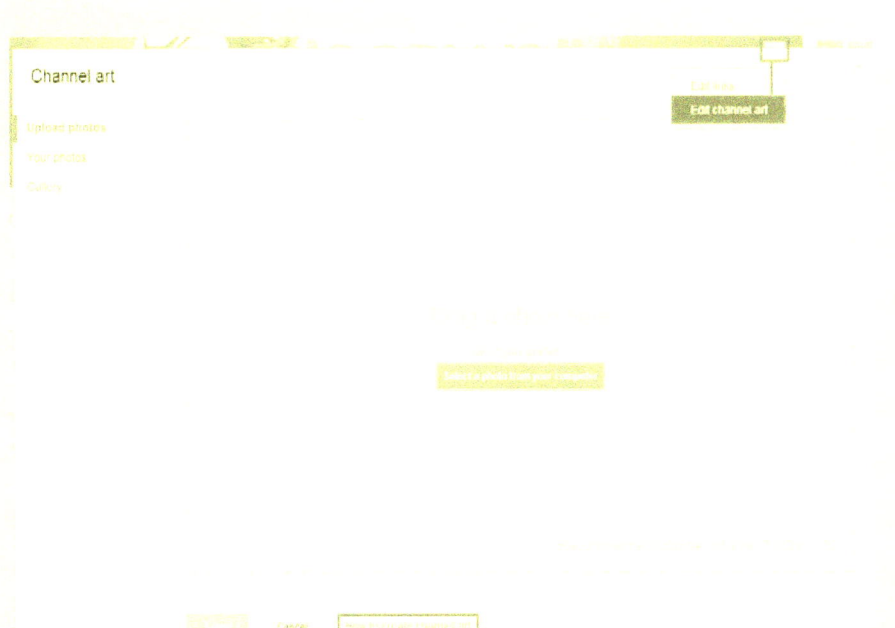

channel tweaking (new)

Going back to click on 'edit links', it will bring the page down a bit and show more areas to input data. The first area is the 'Channel Description', because of the new onechannel layout I would play with the description and text to see how it displays once you are done. Make sure to save your changes before moving on. Below the channel description area is the 'Custom Links' option. Input any none social media URL's you wish to display at the top of your channel's page.

channel tweaking (new)

Finally the social media links, choose how many links you wish to display over your channel's page. Make sure to include every social media widget you have. Social media is a key player in promoting your videos so be sure to have everything organized and configured correctly. The last option is what statistics to display publicly on your channel. There is the option to show your channel views and also the date you joined YouTube. Below is what the social media and custom links will look like on your channel once created and saved.

channel tweaking (new)

Go ahead and view your channel as if you were a viewer and non-subscriber. Open a new browser which you are not signed into Google and view your channel. Pretend to put yourself in the shoes of your audience, what would they like and not like.

The landing video which describes your channel is called the 'Unsubscribed trailer' video. This should be a video where you introduce yourself and give the audience a reason to continue to follow your channel. You can edit the trailer video by clicking on the pencil icon of your channel's home page next to the 'Unsubscribed trailer' text.

channel tweaking (new)

Next you want to explore what's below the trailer video. By default YouTube adds your Recent Uploads & Popular Uploads. Scroll all the way to the bottom and you should see a button that says 'Add a section'. Click on the button to add all sorts of content or playlists to your channels home page. What you do here is up to you. I suggest playing around with the look and feel of these options. Once you are happy with the content now you can organize them to be at the top of your page or at the bottom. To do this, in the top right of a section where the pencil icon is (need to hover in these areas to make the options appear) you will notice an up arrow and down arrow. Click on the arrows to decide which content appears where.

Recent uploads

Popular uploads

YouTube Paycheck ©2013 Author: Corey Flecken

channel tweaking (new)

If you are unsure where to create a playlist, click into your video manager control panel.

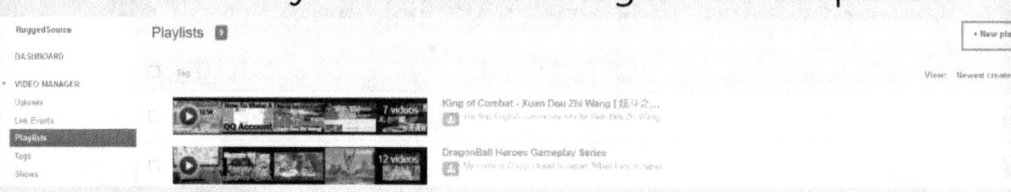

Click on the Playlists tab. YouTube will bring you to your current playlists, if any. To create a list simply click on the 'New playlist' button in the top right. When making playlists try to include a good description for the playlist along with relevant keywords so that you appear within search results.

The last area to edit is the 'About' section. Once again use good keywords based on what your videos are about.

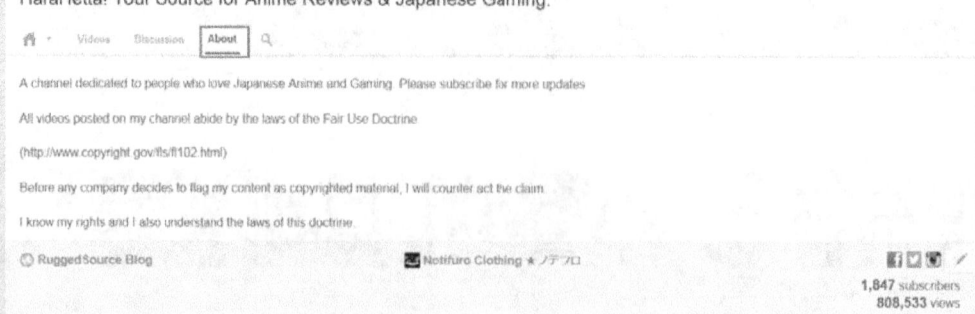

start making money

I figured I would share my most current earnings below (March 2013) while I am in Japan at the time of writing this book. You can see I am averaging $2500 a month. Multiplied by 12 is 30k straight into my bank account. Just by making a video or two a week. If you also have a full time job that is roughly 50k a year, with work and effort using YouTube you could add 10k-100k+ a year to your salary. Even if you started to make the minimum threshold of $100 a month. Don't you think that is great? If your show is about video games and you are making an extra $100 dollars a month, that means you could buy a new video game every month to review and talk about. Return on investment!

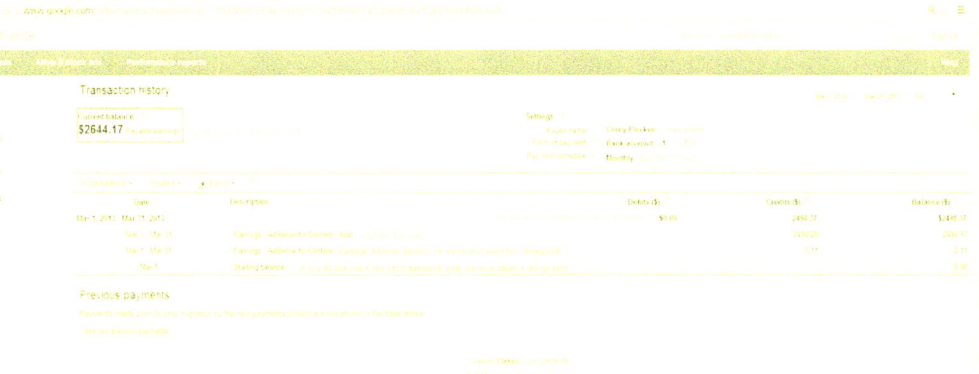

start making money

To start making money with YouTube you need to enable 'monetization' against your account. To do this log into your YouTube account and go to the dashboard. Click into 'channel settings' and you will see a 'Features' option. Or you can just follow the URL: http://www.youtube.com/account_features

From here you will need to click on the 'enable' button. YouTube will bring you to your account status page to ensure you have no strikes against your account to proceed. After this just keep clicking continue or accept until you are done.

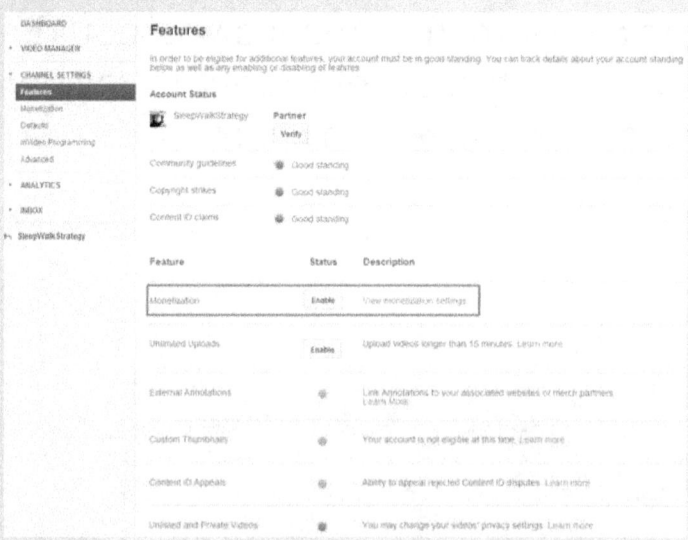

start making money

If you do not have the enable button within the monetization tab there could be several reasons. One, being your YouTube channel is too new. Two, you don't have enough videos or video views. An example on how long you might have to wait is, I uploaded one video which has 77 views and my channel has been active for three weeks. After randomly checking, the enable button appeared. YouTube is very random with this feature, just make sure you do not have any copyright strikes against you account. If you are just starting out, I would make one to three videos and wait a few weeks until the monetization button can be enabled. Then in the interim while you are waiting keep creating content to upload once that option is available. I wouldn't waste any views which could be monetized.

start making money

What does monetization mean exactly for YouTube and my videos? Once your video is uploaded and has been approved for monetization, Google/YouTube will place ads within the video. Most of the time, when you watch a YouTube video, you see a commercial ad then "continue to the video?". This is an example of monetization in action. For more information on monetization and the type of videos which can be enabled to generate revenue can be found here: http://www.youtube.com/account_monetization

After enabling your YouTube account with monetization, the next thing we need to do is sign up for Google AdSense and link the AdSense account with your YouTube channel.

start making money

To sign up with Google AdSense go here:
http://www.google.com/adsense/start/

Please note if you already have an AdSense account associated with another email address, open a new browser window and login there. If you are signing up for the first time, you will be asked to enter your social security number or business EIN number. Then Google will mail you a post card to your address. Once you get the card you can activate your AdSense account.

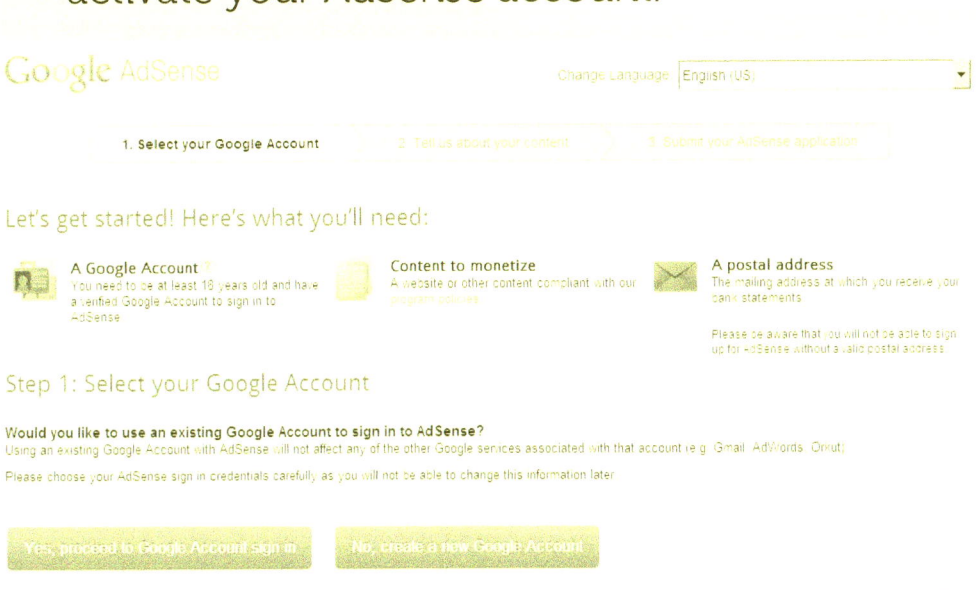

start making money

If your YouTube account is activated for monetization but your Google AdSense account isn't, you will not receive any revenue. This means while you are earning money with your YouTube videos, until you activate your AdSense account you will not be paid. All funds will be kept until then. Once your AdSense account has been activated, you will either get a check from Google or bank deposit of $100+ on a month per month basis.

I created a YouTube video if there are any questions on setting up your AdSense account with YouTube and can be viewed here:

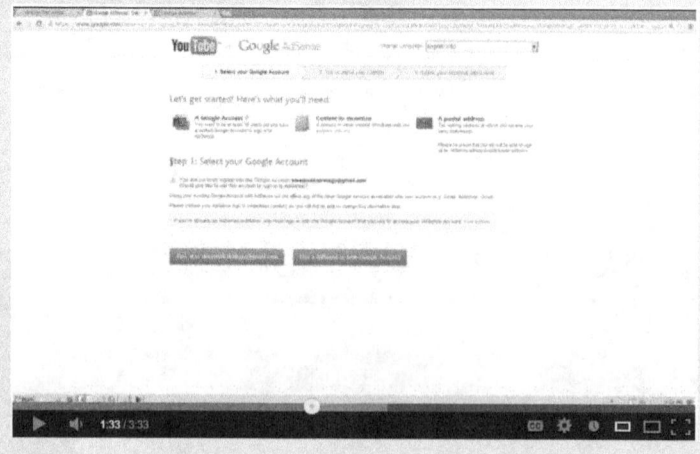

start making money

After all said and done we need to now turn on the money making option for our videos! Log into YouTube and go to the video manager. Within your uploads section, you should now see a new icon with a dollar sign '$' shown below:

Click on this new button and it will bring you to the monetization options for your videos. Check off the tick box next to 'Monetize my video'. A popup might occur expressing to confirm you own all of the rights to this video and cannot earn money if you do not, etc. You want the 'Monetize with Ads' option enabled. Within the ad formats option, select the first two.

Overlay: Popup banners during your video.
TrueView: Commercial Ad's before your video.

start making money

The syndication option is to show your video on all platforms (PC, tablet, phone, etc.) or only if the user can see an advertisement. If the user can not see an advertisement, when they are attempting to view the video a message might appear expressing 'This video can not be played on this device'. Now I have thought about this and wasn't sure which is the best option. If a user can not click an ad on my videos I can not make money but at the same time I could be losing views and subscribers. I feel views and subscribers are more important for shows starting out. Once you reach 50k subscribers, I would then switch this option and rake in tons of cash.

start making money

After enabling a video to be monetized you might see the dollar sign icon has become green. If the '$' symbol is not white and is green, this means your video is under review by the YouTube team to confirm it can be monetized.

This has become more frequent with YouTube when trying to monetize videos just uploaded. Sometimes going into the video and watching it fully and going back several times will activate the monetization. I have had to wait several weeks at times until they have passed review. Your last option is to remove the video and re-upload it under a different name and to put garbled text in the video name and description until it is fully monetized. After that change back all of the values correctly for the title, description and keyword. I found using Google Chrome's incognito mode works best for this.

start making money

Verifying your YouTube account as a 'Partner'. Within the dashboard of YouTube and in the Channel Settings > Features tab, under your account status section. There is your 'Partner' status. You will need to verify your YouTube account to continue.

Once you click on the 'Verify' button it will ask you how do you want to verify your account. Google will either send you a text message or call your phone giving you a 5 digit code. After your have submitted the code your YouTube account has been verified.

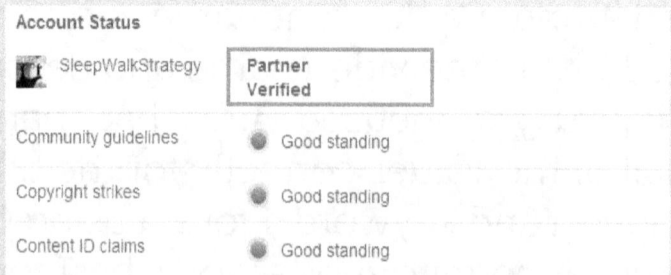

earning views

After enabling Adsense for your channel, you will discover a new option under the 'Analytics' menu titled **Earnings reports**. Under the 'earnings reports' header you will notice:
Estimated Earnings Ad Performance

The estimated earnings area provides earning related details for the four partner content types. Channel and video levels are displayed as well.

Total estimated earnings:

Net revenue from all Google-sold advertising sources for the selected date range and region.

Ad Earnings: **AdSense earnings**

Estimated earnings from auction-sold advertising via AdSense for the selected date range and region.

DoubleClick earnings:

Estimated earnings from reserved-sold advertising via DoubleClick (DCLK) and other YouTube-sold sources for the selected date range and region.

earning views

Transactions:

Revenue derived from YouTube Rentals, which are available for select Partners.

Log into your Google Adsense account to view the estimated earnings on there too. You will see when your next check or direct deposit from your earnings will be sent.

Some earnings will not appear right away in your account and will take YouTube up to 3-7 days for the correct information to be gathered and computed by their system.

tracking analytics

Using your analytical data is useful to help gain more views, subscribers, followers, etc. However, the stats are only useful once you have collected data over a period of time. If you are just starting out the data will not be as useful to you as it would several months down the line. However I will discuss what to look for and a few techniques you can use to benefit your channel with the analytics.

Once you are logged into your YouTube channel, go to the dashboard or video manager. From there you will see an 'Analytics' tab under the 'Channel Settings' tab, click on this. You will be automatically brought to the overview of your channels analytical data. This is the past 30 days of stats. Also note that data for the current day takes 24 hours to update and sometimes even longer. If you gain an excessive amount of views in one day, YouTube will take several days to process this data into your charts.

tracking analytics

The overview page is semi-useful showing nice charts and graphs along with your estimated earnings from your YouTube videos.

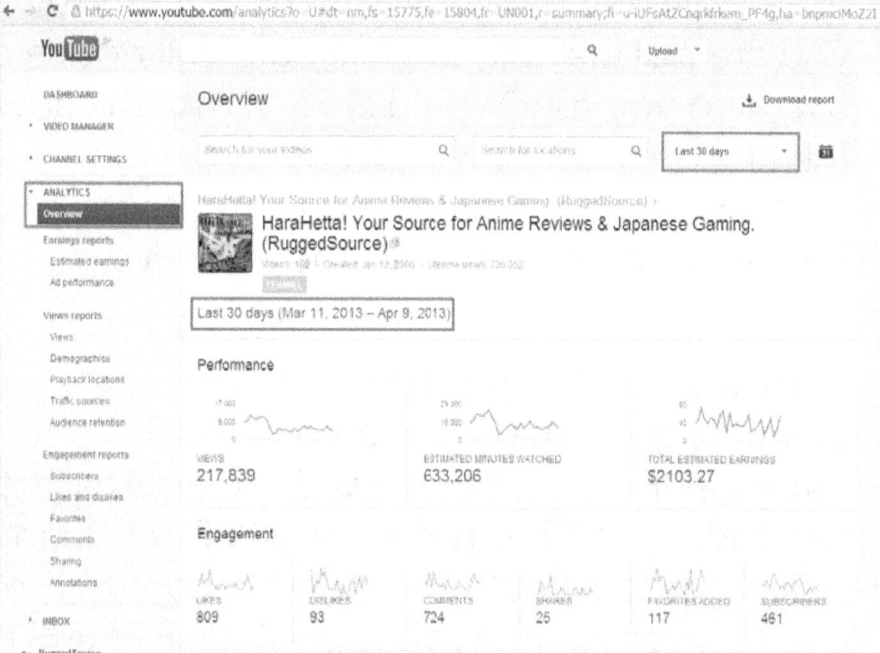

You can change the overview's stats by changing the date range from 'Last 30 Days' to a custom range. I always like to use the 'Current Month' stats to see how well I am performing.

tracking analytics

You can also click on one of the graphs and it will bring you into the pages overview of statistics. The most important graphs will be the 'Engagement' section. The more users view and comment on your videos, theoretically you should make more money. Remember I expressed it is important to catch a user's attention and utilize annotations within your videos for comments, subscriptions and likes? Well this will show you if your annotations is working. Below the engagement graphs is your YouTube's top 10 most viewed videos for the current date selection chosen above. All the way near the bottom is two pie chart sections. You have your demographics which shows where in the world are your visitors coming from. Lastly, your discovery - how viewers are finding your YouTube videos. This is the second most important stats you will want to study with your videos and analytics.

tracking analytics

Quick review on the key areas of your analytical data and the details in which you should be paying close attention to. First being the **engagement** section.

Second being the **discovery** section.

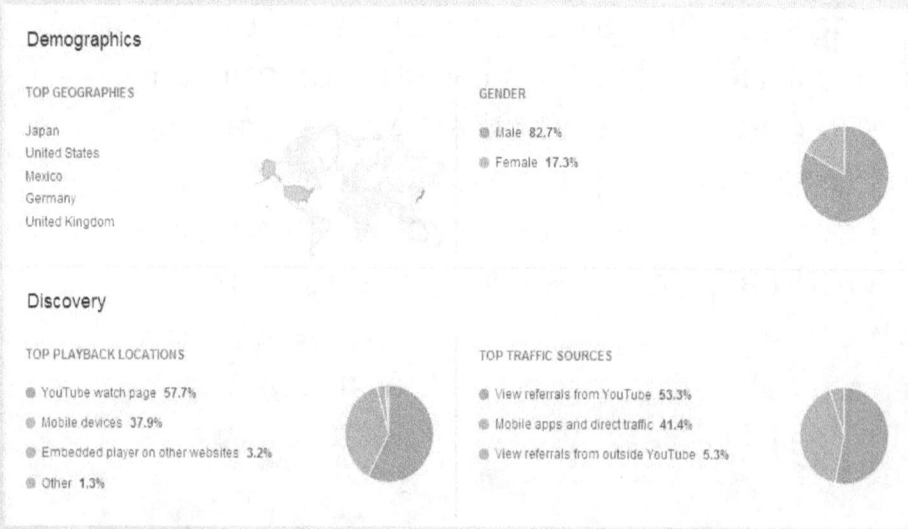

tracking analytics

When going over the data take notes. I like to use a notebook and pen. When I write down information it stays in my head better. This also allows me to read it later on to figure out certain strategies to promote my videos. Your goal is to find trends within your videos. Why did this video have 4000 views during the first week of March. It is possible that a blog posted your video on their site and that is why your video gained so many views during that week of March.

I will show you a case study on one of my videos which was posted on a blog and how to find out this data.

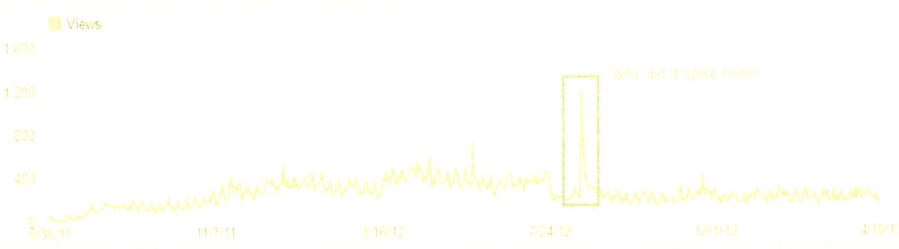

tracking analytics

Within the overview page of the analytics area, within the top 10 video section click into one of your videos. This will bring you into the stats for this video itself. YouTube will also populate the 'Search for your videos' section for this video. Remember to 'x' it out to get back to the main overview section.

Change the date range to 'lifetime', you will want to see any spikes since your video was posted. This is located next to the 'Search for locations' box. Click on the current settings or dates and a drop down menu will appear. At the bottom of the list will be 'Lifetime'. See the image above for where to change this. YouTube might take some time to refresh the page's data if your channel has a lot of data or if the video itself has a ton of information to reset.

tracking analytics

With the data now refreshed to the lifetime stats, try to notice any similar spikes within the graphs. Write down any similarities you might see. Then go into the 'views' graph (click on it).

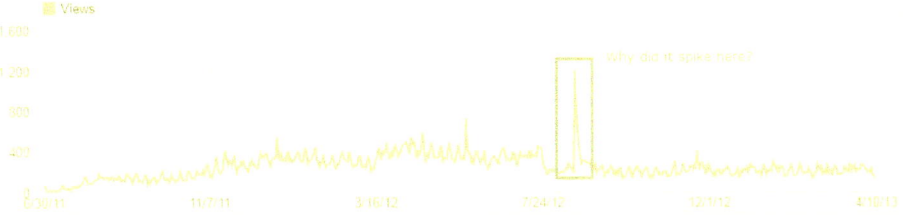

I posted this example earlier and you can see for a few days that my video had a spike in views compared to the reset of the days. We need to find out why. In your menu to the left, click on 'playback locations'. You will see the spike is also there.

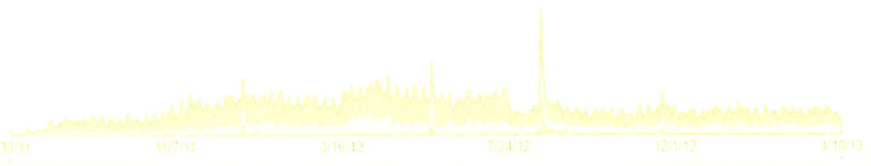

tracking analytics

Under your graph you will see a date range and white sliders on the left and right side of your timeline. Drag those sliders just before and after the spike(s) of your stats.

This will change your video stats below. We want to see the 'playback location' data more precisely. You will see that the orange spike is close to being the blue spike. When looking at the playback location data below, the orange spike is embedded sources. This means someone took my video and posted it on their site.

☑	PLAYBACK LOCATION	VIEWS ↓
☑	● YouTube watch page	2,610 (50.0%)
☑	● Embedded player on other websites	1,626 (31.2%)
☑	● Mobile devices	955 (18.3%)
☑	● YouTube channel page	25 (0.5%)

tracking analytics

Let's find out which site posted my video. You will notice that the 'Embedded player on other websites' text is clickable. After clicking on this link, it will bring you deeper into your video's stats on who/where it is being hosted and viewed. As you can see in the image below:

	PLAYBACK LOCATION	VIEWS ↓
☑	saiyanisland.com	1,153 (70.9%)
☑	guiamania.com	163 (10.0%)
☑	nintendo-difference.com	59 (3.6%)
☑	otakufreaks.com	37 (2.3%)
☑	amha.fr	35 (2.2%)
☑	meristation.com	27 (1.7%)
☑	facebook.com	21 (1.3%)
☑	nextn.es	21 (1.3%)
☑	bing.com	11 (0.7%)
☑	googleusercontent.com	11 (0.7%)

For this one video a website titled 'saiyanisland.com' hosted my video causing the spike in views. This is GREAT data and you should be writing anything like this down.

tracking analytics

Why is this data so important? Because now what you are going to do is reach out to the website owners in this list. Like I mentioned before write the data down and go to the websites in the list. Try to find a contact section for these sites and email the website content creators. Express that you saw that they posted your video on their site and ask if they could post other videos you have on their site or ask them what kind of footage they would want that they would re-post on their site. This is one of the most beneficial techniques you can use to promote your channel. You want to build a following for your channel, almost like a family or cult. A group of people that love you and will watch every video you post more than once and share your videos on their social media pages to their other friends. More information on playback location data from YouTube can be found here: https://support.google.com/youtube/bin/answer.py?hl=en&answer=1714546

tracking analytics

Next we want to click on the 'traffic sources' menu option from the left navigation area. This will pull in data on how the viewer found your video. Very similar to 'playback locations' but instead of coding the video to be played on a blog or site, the blogger posted a URL to your video instead. Get ready to write down more data to study and act upon. Below is an example from one of my videos:

TRAFFIC SOURCE	VIEWS
Embedded player (unknown sources)	1,626 (31.2%)
YouTube search	1,329 (25.5%)
Mobile apps and direct traffic (unknown sources)	1,167 (22.4%)
YouTube suggested video	457 (8.8%)
External website	369 (7.1%)
Google search	182 (3.5%)
YouTube - other features	55 (1.1%)
Homepage feeds and subscriptions	28 (0.5%)
YouTube channel page	3 (0.1%)

tracking analytics

As you can see I highlighted the 'external website' option. You want to click into this option and view the data there. Google will most likely be at the top of the list but then below that will be websites that are sharing your videos. Once again you will record the website information and go to them later and try to contact the owners on posting your videos more often, etc. You want as much traffic as possible. By interacting with other website users, you increase the chances that they will tweet your videos to their followers. This is the kind of free advertising you want because in the end it makes you more money with monetization views.

TRAFFIC SOURCE	VIEWS
Google	162 (43.9%)
mynintendonews.com	110 (29.8%)
elotrolado.net	30 (8.1%)
facebook.com	23 (6.2%)
neogaf.com	15 (4.1%)

tracking analytics

'Audience retention' is the next stat we will be discussing and it can be the most brutal and discouraging data against your videos. However, you need to push aside your ego and figure out what you are doing wrong. You want your viewers to stay on your videos as long as possible. If you are getting 10k+ views a day but your viewers are leaving after 10 seconds of watching that does nothing for you. In this section, you'll be able to determine where your viewers are dropped per video. Below is an example from one of my videos. It is a long video over 10 minutes which is bad in itself. You really should not have a video over 5 minutes.

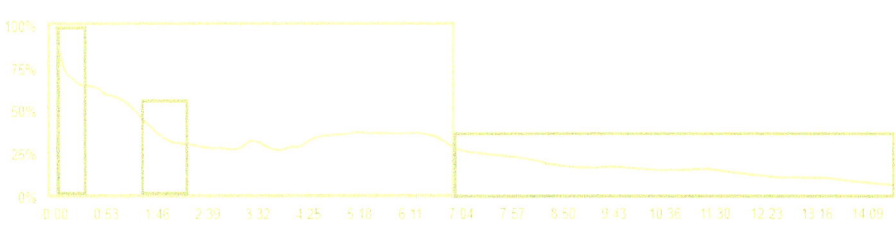

tracking analytics

I say this because the average attention span for a viewer is 3-5 minutes on YouTube. This is why shows like '=3' perform so well due to the show only being 3 minutes long. It is short and keeps the viewer's attention span before they become uninterested. Don't worry, you will get use to doing this as you practice every week. Remember, practice makes perfect and although no one is perfect, you want to aim high. Going back to my chart from the previous page you will see that within the first 3 minutes I have a decent drop off rate. What does this tell me? It tells me that I have to work on keeping my audiences attention in the beginning of my videos. I need to spark their brains with a 'feature' that I will show in my video later on so that they keep watching until that 'feature' appears. It's also important to study the other parts of the video where users drop off. Try to put yourself in a viewer's position and see whether or not your video falls short in keeping someone engaged.

join a youtube network

Before jumping into joining a YouTube network I would like to answer a few questions.

-Q: What is a YouTube network?
-A: YouTube's network is essentially a community/studio ran by a certain company that hosts and promotes original YouTube content.

-Q: Why join a network?
-A: When you join a network, you gain access to additional additional features within YouTube that help promote your channel and videos. Additionally, the network should promote your videos as well. Sometimes networks have a higher pay rate than Google Adsense does.

-Q: How do networks make money?
-A: They control the advertisements displayed on your videos.

join a youtube network

Don't jump into joining a network. Start looking for a network once they start to find you. This will happen. Once you start to reach a certain amount of daily views, subscribers, etc. Network scouts will start to personally message you via YouTube. When this happens, you know you have something valuable. Remember the networks want your content, you have something they want. Do not sign the first contract you receive. I have seen many YouTube content creators get the shaft after signing a contract and it's terrible. It is like how the "Beach Boys" sold all of their music rights away and do not collect any royalties from what they created. You do not want this to happen. Networks will help you as long as it helps them. They are a business and in the business world, it's about making money. You have ownership to the content that they need to make revenue. If they don't have content they will go out of business, remember this.

join a youtube network

As I stated earlier, never sign the first contract you get. I will admit, it is exciting the first time a network is interested in your videos. Something inside of you will want to sign the contract right away thinking it will be lost if you don't. This is not the case. For every contract you get, do the following: send a reply email and ask a few questions. Notice how long it takes for the network to get back to you and if it is an automated response. I have found that it takes an average of about seven business days for a network to response to an email. This should calm your nerves and make you realize that you're not as "special" to them as they'd like you to think. Although you are unique and can bring something to the table, it's important to remember that you're not their sole focus. At the same time don't fret that you are not special because you are, it just shows you the reality of it all and how it is a business more than anything. Have a lawyer review your contract, I have seen some contracts sneaking in that if you create a new YouTube show while in contract the network has the right to use it.

join a youtube network

Another sneaky clause is that if you create a video that causes any legal issues, you will need to reimburse the network for lawyer fee's. We all know how expensive lawyer fee's can be so things like this needs to be addressed and reassured before signing any contract. Do not be afraid to challenge a contract either. It is normal to amend contracts, it'll show businesses that you're knowledgeable and can't be taken advantage of.

Few acronyms which you should know:
CPM: Cost Per Mille (Thousand Impressions)
CPA: Cost Per Action
CPV: Cost Per Visitor or Cost Per View
CPC: Cost Per Conversion or Cost Per Click

When joining a network try to find the best CPM rate. Try to get over $5 per thousand impressions. Think about it, if your channel is

join a youtube network

getting three thousand views a day, that's $15 guaranteed per day you will be earning. Multiply that by 30 days in a month and you get $450 on top of the other bonuses with your network. I average 3k-4k views per day and this is growing every time I upload a new video. Luckily my CPM is $8 and earn about $30 per day just on impression views. That is close to $1000 per month. You too can do this, it all depends on how well you manage your videos and social media.

Try not to sign into a two year contract. The internet changes so fast that two years or more will feel like forever. Shoot for a one year or breakable contract at a month's notice. I know for myself I was approached by TGN (The Gamers Network) – At the time their contract allowed me to leave at any time but with a month's notice. No lock in contracts are great.

join a youtube network

Try to use the entertainment guidelines with percentages as a starting point when looking at the contract details. Even though online media networks are still fairly new, the business of "vultures taking a cut from talent" is not. In the world of entertainment, agents take 10%-15% and managers take 10%-15%. What you are doing is very similar so should be treated near so. What your network is bringing to the table will scale the percents differently. An example is a network offering to re-do your videos with special graphics and effects, making your show more eye catching. Or if your network is offering to help with directing and acting, etc. As a result, the network's rates will change accordingly to these options.

Finally, after reading everything above and having lawyers involved, review the networks. Find a content creator currently in contract

join a youtube network

with the network you're considering and ask them questions. Try not to get in too much detail because there could be some legal issues when asking but just see if they are happy and if they could re-sign a contract who would it be with?

In the realm of analytics the reason why a network will start to reach out to you is for one of two reasons. One, being that you have accumulated a decent subscriber base and daily view count. Two, if your show has quality and potential. Now the number two option is very rare. Don't worry about this option just yet, I would focus on gaining subscribers and viewers. In order to keep track and create goals, I would suggest using the website 'Social Blade'. Social Blade is an online YouTube channel data collecting tool available to anyone at anytime. The only thing is you need to enter your channel in first to start collecting data.

join a youtube network

To do this go to: http://www.socialblade.com/ and enter your channel name into the stat searching tool. If you only see one record and

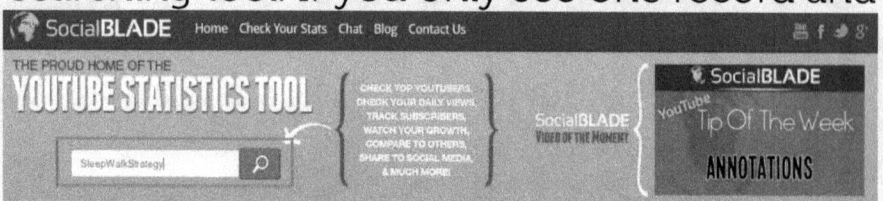

that is today's date, this is the first time you or anyone else has wanted to see your stats. Everyday check your Social Blade stats to see how your channel is progressing along with looking at your YouTube analytical data. Once you start gaining over a thousand views per day, this is usually when a network will start to contact you. Most networks study the Social Blade stats of channels to determine if a show is growing faster than expected. This is when they try and snake them into contacts.

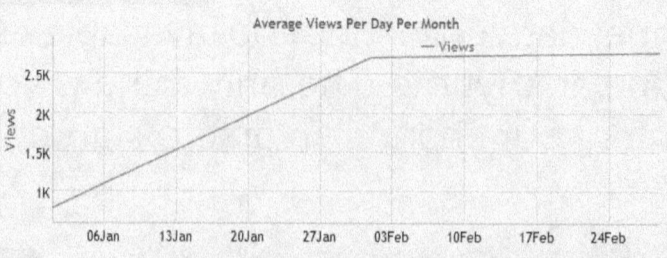

join a youtube network

As you can see within Social Blade, my anime/game channel has a rank of 'B'. When compared to other related channels I am up against, my channel is growing faster and has a better rank. At the time of writing this book, I

get about three YouTube network emails per week. Expressing my channel would be great for their network. Another reason why not to sign too early. I was so excited when I received my first contact from a YouTube network. It was a personal email from Blip.TV expressing how they truly they loved my show. More emails were sent back and forth but I ended up with a different network.

join a youtube network

Do your research on networks before joining! Below are a few example networks to look into. Note that the Makers Studios network is a multi-level network. Under Makers Studios is the [RPM network](). The RPM network then has cousin networks, so you will see a lot of contract being titled something like 'XYZ part of RPM Networks'.

Also some networks want your show directly on their network and to be removed from YouTube. Such network examples are Vevo and Blip.tv – Be careful what kind of network you choose because while the CPM might be more for a network that doesn't focus on YouTube. A network allowing you to continue to use YouTube will generate more views with a lower CPM rate. Example:

Private: CPM $10 but you only get 1k per day now.
Public: CPM $5 but you get 3k per day as usual.

join a youtube network

Below are a list of the top and most common networks. You can get more information on other networks at Social Blade (http://socialblade.com/youtube/top/networks).

RPM Network: http://partner.makerstudios.com

Full Screen: http://fullscreen.net/creators

Maker Studios:
http://www.makerstudios.com/join/

The Game Station:
https://partner.thegamestation.com/

The Game Network: http://tgn.tv/join-tgn/

Alloy Digital:
http://www.alloydigital.com/partnership/

success

I wish you the best of luck on creating your own YouTube channel and videos. Hopefully, after reading this book, you've gained a better perspective on how to achieve your goals. I'm happy to help anyone I can so please do not hesitate to contact me. Just note with my schedule and priorities it will take me some time to answer everyone's questions.

I did not become successful overnight. It took hard work and dedication to achieve the views and subscribers throughout my channels. You can do this too! I guarantee it. Start off slow by posting an episode once a week. Learn video and editing techniques. Make sure you are up to date on trends and what is popular for your subject. After several months you will start to notice you are earning more money. This will give you the drive you need to become more successful with your YouTube channel.

Remember to create a blog or website for your subscribers to follow.

success

Ensure you connect all social media aspects to your videos. At the end of this book, I have created a To-Do List to aid you on your adventure.

After seeing a network, whether it be Google or YouTube, deposit your first paycheck into your bank account (I use direct deposit) you will feel very excited. You will have just earned extra money by making a video. The concept is mind-blowing but is true.

The following chapters are bonus chapters as needed. Which will aid you through your YouTube progression. After setting up your channel and creating a routine for yourself come back to the bonus chapters when required.

I have also include a glossary of sites at the end of the book that can benefit you.

video game recording

Recording video games on your PC can be a bit different from using Camtasia to record 'How To' videos or PC actions. This method is only good for PC users, unfortunately the developers which created the software has only made it for Windows and not a MAC machine.

You will need to download the software called 'Fraps'. Visit their website here:
http://www.fraps.com/download.php

Fraps will install (by default) on the same level as your C:\ drive usually - C:\Fraps

After installing, find the icon to load Fraps. You can play around with the additional settings the software has to offer but at the moment we are only concerned with the 'General' & 'Movies' tabs.

video game recording

Fraps will load the 'General' tab by default. Between the five options you have below you want to only have the following enabled:

-Fraps window always on top
-Display status on LCD

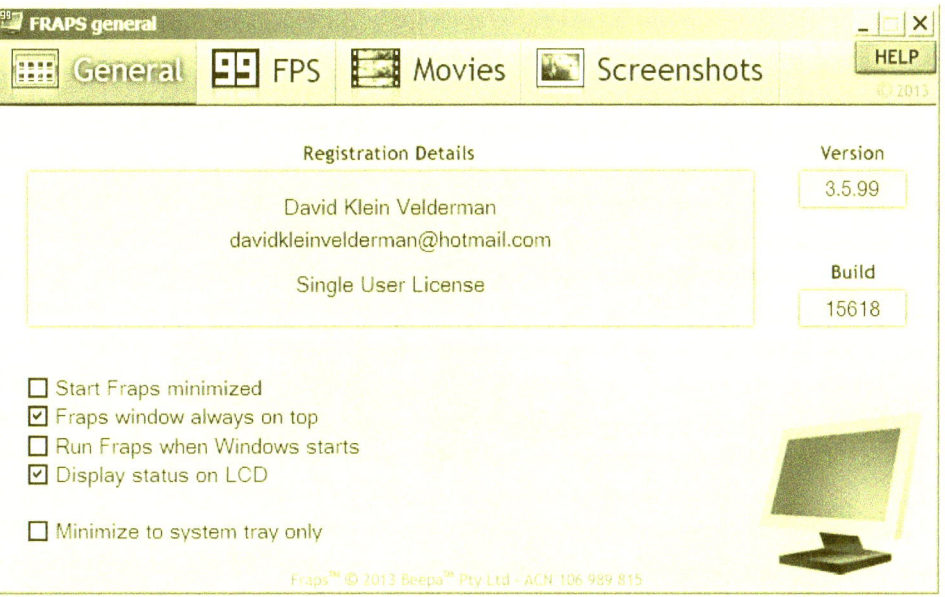

video game recording

Next click on the 'Movies' tab in the top navigation. Usually, by default all of the settings should match my image below. However, I do suggest testing the *Video Capture Settings* while recording your videos.

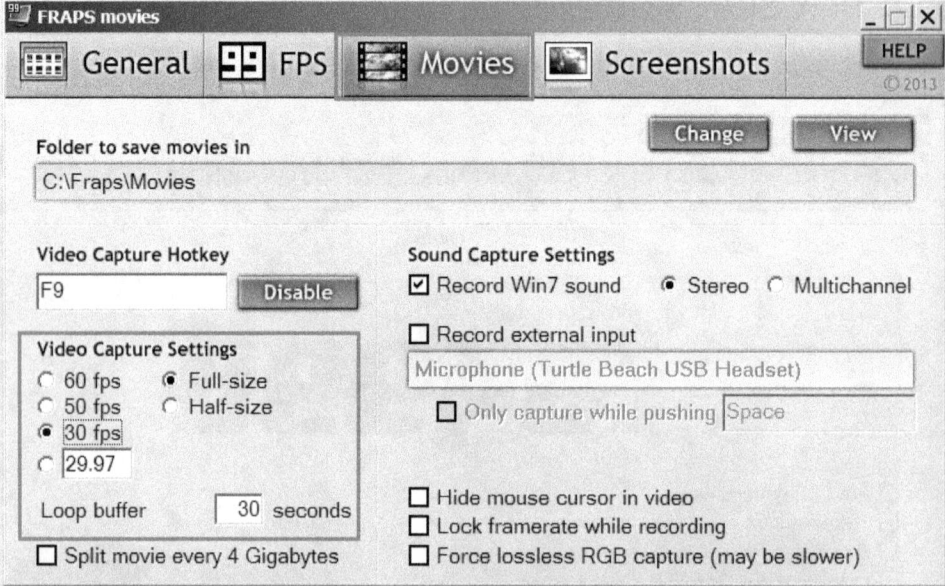

After you have the correct options and settings enabled, just minimize the Fraps program.

video game recording

All you need to do now is load any game you wish to record. Once the game is loaded you will notice a RED number spiking randomly in the top left of the game window.

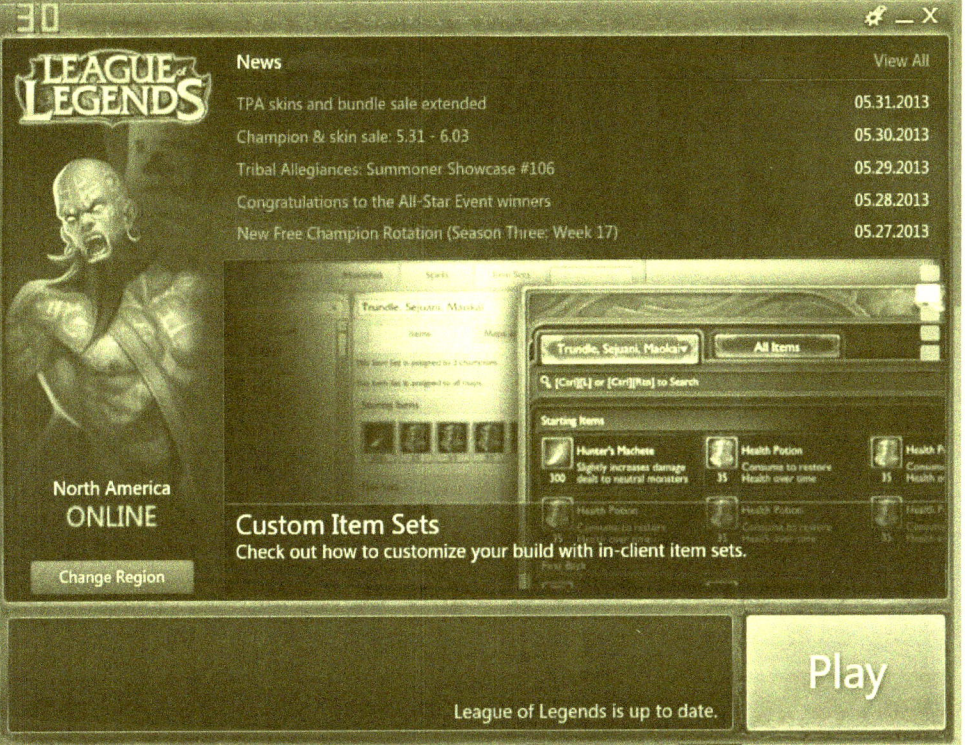

This means Fraps is running and is ready to start recording your game play.

video game recording

To start your game play recording just press the 'F9' key on your keyboard. The red number in the top left should now be YELLOW. This means Fraps is working and recording. To stop your recording just press 'F9' again and the numbers will change back to red.

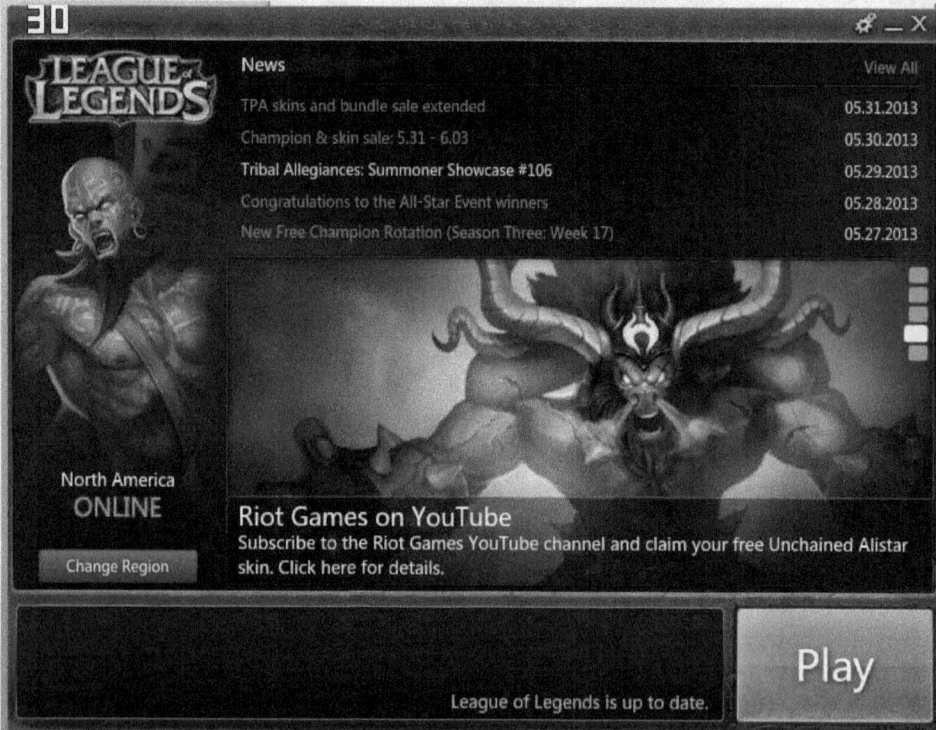

Red = Off / Yellow = On

video game recording

One thing to note is the video files Fraps records are very large. A one minute video could be around 2gb. It is very easy to forget Fraps is recording and your hard drive space alerts you there is no more left. Do some test recordings with the settings before fully diving into creating videos.

After you have your game recordings, it is always good to add voice narration. This is usually a must when you're in contract with a YouTube network. By default game footage can be claimed as copyright by the game developers if no voice narration is with the game footage.

There are two ways you can do this. My personal preference is bringing the video footage into Camtasia Studio. Within Camtasia there is an option to voice record over video footage.

video game recording

Once you have Camtasia loaded, import your video file(s). From the top menu go to: Tools > Voice narration... (seen below)

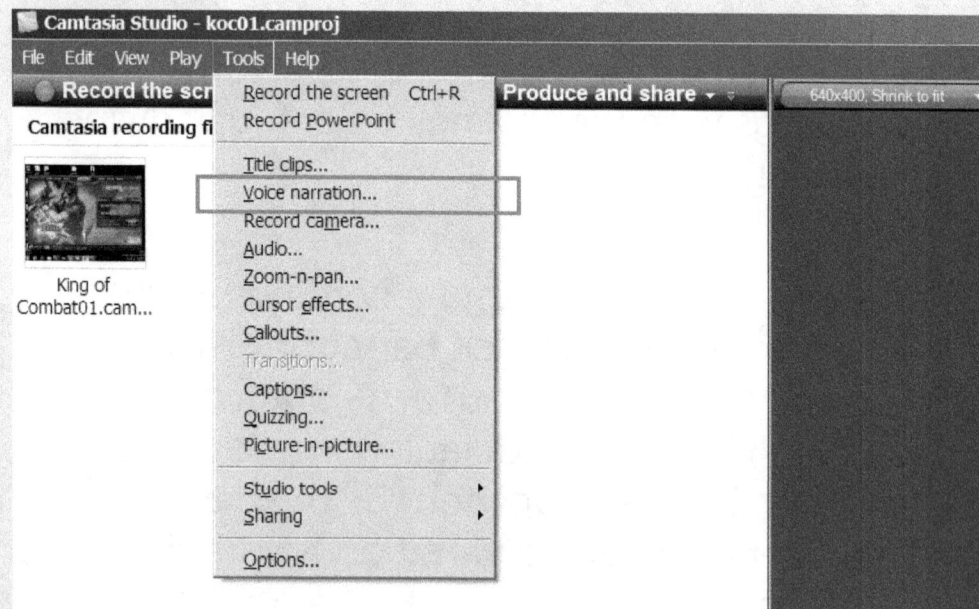

This will open a new window dialogue to record over your video footage and create a new audio layer once it's done so it is not merged with any other audio.

video game recording

The second method to voice narrate over your footage is to use the free software called 'Audacity' which can be downloaded from here: http://audacity.sourceforge.net/

You can also use Audacity within Sony Vegas Pro as a noise filter reduction.

You can actually run 'Audacity' at the same time you are recording your game play footage with Fraps.

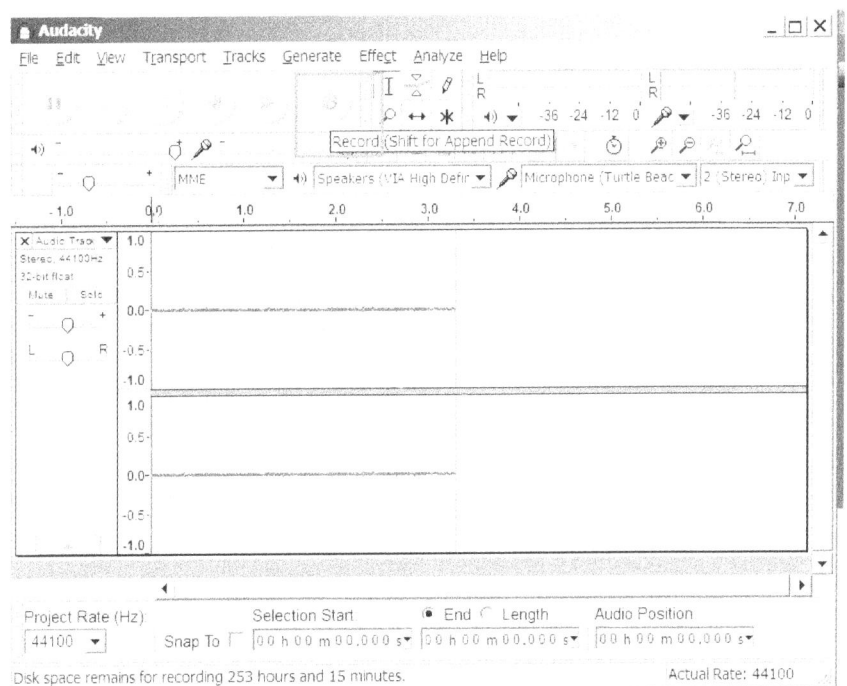

video game recording

After 'Audacity' is installed, click the icon to load it. Once loaded, just press the red record button near the top. You will notice the program will start to record audio. Depending if you have two or more microphone options, this will need to be managed via the mid menu with drop downs selecting which microphone to use for the recording.

Now you can either voice narrate during or after your game play and save the audio file. Once this has been done, you will need to import both files (video & audio) into another video editing software (Camtasia, Sony Vegas, etc.) to match them via layers and render your footage for YouTube.

how to live stream

To LIVE stream on YouTube you will need to be part of a network and also have a certain amount of views/subscribers to unlock this feature. Therefore, this chapter will explain how to LIVE stream with YouTube and also a site such as Twitch (http://www.twitch.tv/). You can use sites like Twitch to bring traffic to your YouTube channel with banner ads or text, linking viewers to your YouTube channel.

Below are a few sites where you can LIVE stream from:

Twitch: http://www.twitch.tv/
USTREAM: http://www.ustream.tv/
Live Stream: http://new.livestream.com/
Justin: http://www.justin.tv/
*YouTube LIVE: http://www.youtube.com/live/

how to live stream

To LIVE Stream from YouTube, log into your account and go to the video manager section. In the left hand menu under the dashboard, you will notice a 'Live Events' option. Click on this feature and YouTube will bring you to your 'live events' page. It will list any scheduled live events you might have. If this is your first time creating a live event it will be empty. In the top right of the page there will be a button to allow you to create a 'New live event'.

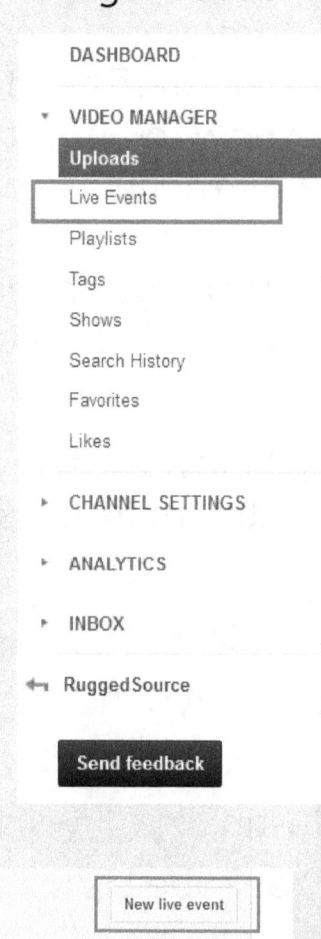

how to live stream

Make sure your event is marked as unlisted if this is your first time using the live event option. YouTube can revoke your live stream access if you fail to produce quality live stream events.

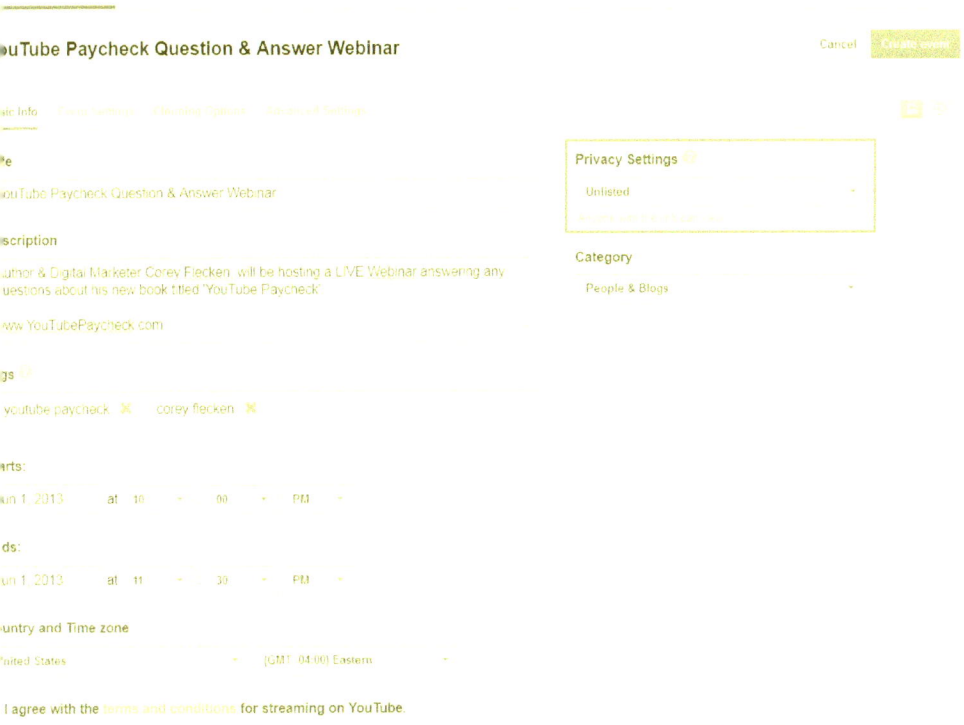

Proceed to enter in the corresponding details into the fields describing your live event.

how to live stream

Once all of the information has been added, continue by clicking on the blue button 'create event' in the top right. The next page you will be able to upload a custom thumbnail of your live event along with selecting the bitrate your stream will be encoded at. After your bitrate has been chosen, you will then need to select your encoder.

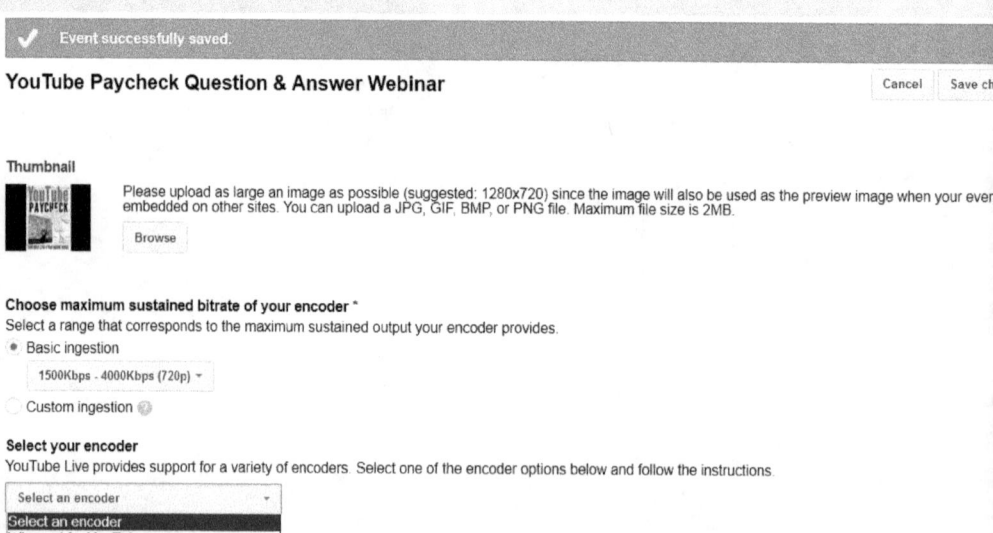

how to live stream

What is an Encoder?

An encoder is a piece of software that enables you to live stream from your computer onto a network such as YouTube, Twitch.tv, etc.

-Adobe has a free encoder called 'Flash Media Live Encoder' which can be downloaded here: http://www.adobe.com/products/flash-media-encoder.html
-Another free encoder is the 'OBS Project': http://obsproject.com/

Paid encoders I recommend are either XSplit or Wirecast.

XSplit: http://www.xsplit.com/
Wirecast: http://www.telestream.net/

how to live stream

I would download a few of the encoders to test them all out. You might end up liking a paid version that could offer more features.

After updating the 'Ingestion Settings' and saving your details. Go back to the 'Info and Settings' tab. You will want to enable several other options within the sub menu tabs. Within the 'Event Settings' section enable the 'Promotions' tick box.

YouTube Paycheck Question & Answer Webinar

Basic Info | **Event Settings** | Claiming Options | Advanced Settings

Recording
- Enable (Maximum 4 hours)
- Disable (Video will not be automatically recorded)

DVR
- ✓ Enable DVR (Maximum 36-hour DVR window)

Broadcast delay
30 seconds

Promotions
- ✓ Promote through InVideo Programming when event is live.

how to live stream

The promotions box allows for a popup to be displayed on your channel's videos during your LIVE stream, expressing you are hosting an event. The other options are more for user preference. I have included what I would normally choose for a live event in the image above.

In the 'Claiming Options' you will want to enable the claim. Doing this will grant advertisements during your LIVE stream and by earning revenue with your network.

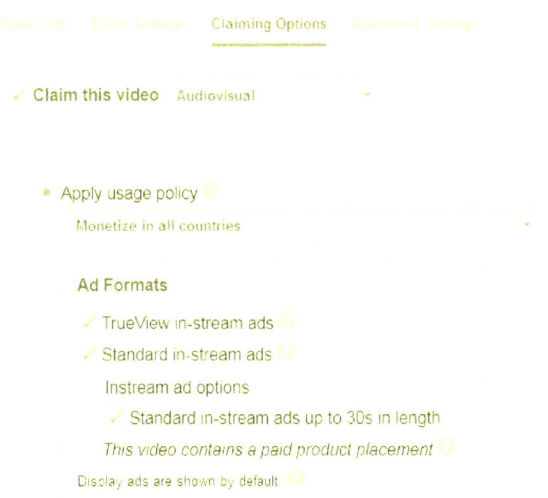

how to live stream

To start your broadcast you will need to enable your encoder to start the stream. Once you have done this go to the 'Live Control Room' tab within the YouTube event section. YouTube will know if your encoder is streaming or not. Any warning will appear in red or orange at the top of the page. If there are no warnings you should see a stream status of GOOD.

YouTube Paycheck Question & Answer Webinar

| Start Encoder | Preview Stream | You're Live! |

▶ Preview   00:00:00

STREAM STATUS	June 2, 2013 03:00 AM (EDT)		AVERAGE LIVE VIEW DURATION	00:00
GOOD	The health is good		TOTAL VIEW TIME (HOURS)	0
240P STREAM			PEAK CONCURRENT	0

Manage   Analytics

Now you need to preview your stream. Above the GOOD status is a blue 'preview' button with a white play icon. Click on this and YouTube will prepare your LIVE stream preview. This can take a few minutes to load.

how to live stream

Once the preview option has finished it will change to 'start encoder'. When you enable the start encoder button, your stream will start to broadcast. During the broadcast YouTube might alert you if your stream is dropping frame rates or if the audio is bad, etc. Just be aware of these alerts and also if possible, view your stream on another computer at the same time to get an idea of what your users are currently experiencing.

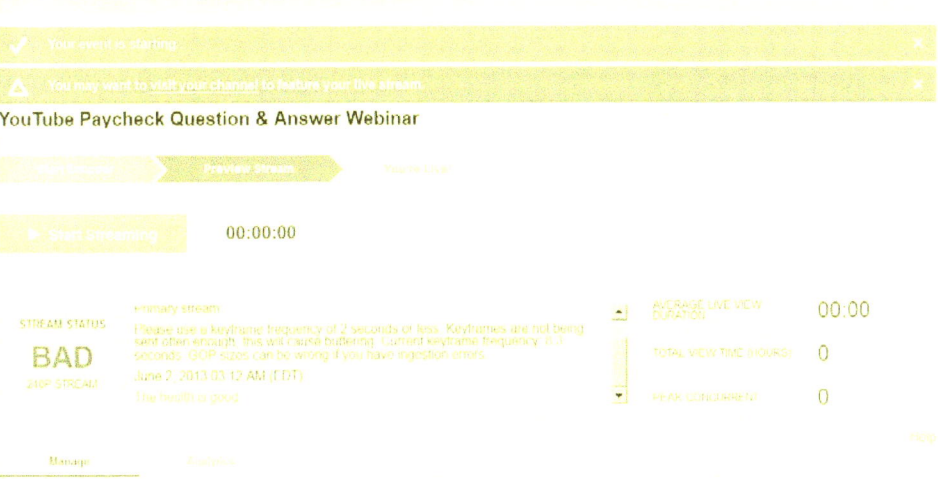

When you stop the stream in YouTube you can not easily re-start it. Either pause or stop the stream from your encoder if needed.

how to live stream

Below is an example of using the YouTube RTMP url data and an encoder. Just copy and paste the details into the matching fields and save.

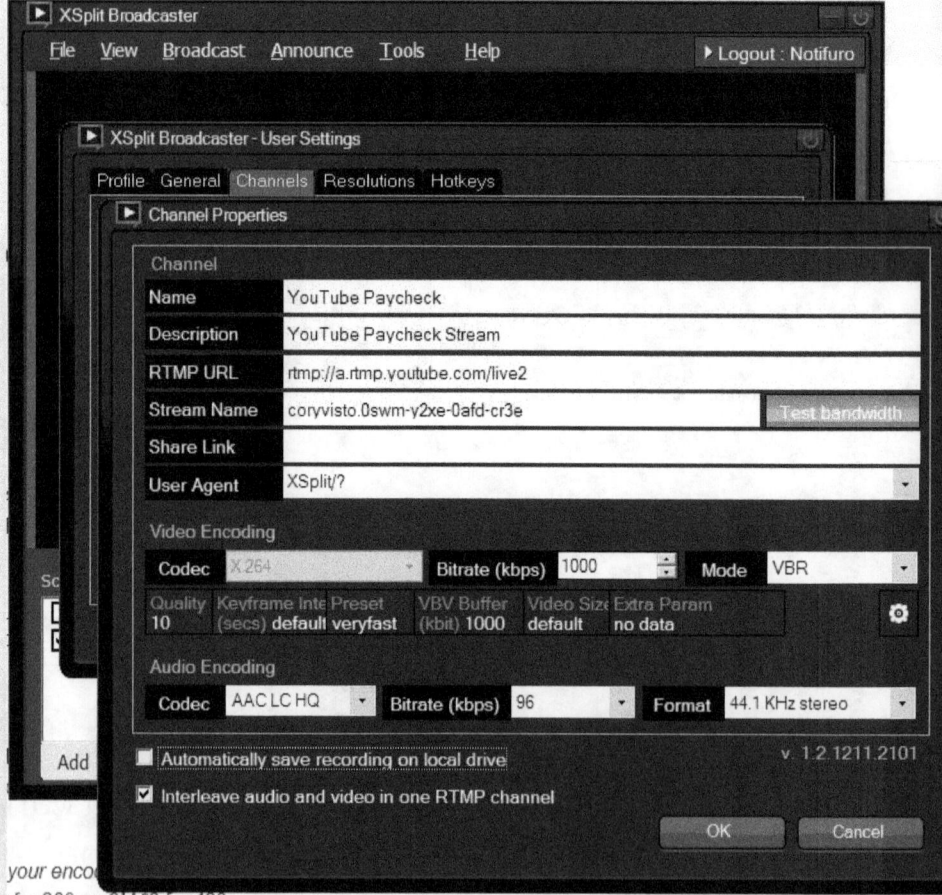

how to live stream

For more information on setting up your encoder to match with YouTube please use the support doc on Google which can be found using this URL: http://goo.gl/RbClP

As I stated earlier, most users will not have the option to LIVE stream with YouTube for awhile. However, don't let this stop you from trying to stream with other platforms. You can always link your stream from Twitch.tv to your YouTube channel. Secondly, most streaming sites allow you to save your broadcast on their site. Then you can download it and upload it to YouTube.

Always think outside the box, use Skype and a LIVE stream site to host interviews with certain people. Broadcast special events or even How To's, create a sense of reality with your viewers.

custom youtube buttons

Ever watch a video on YouTube and you can interact with it by pressing buttons on the video itself? Then when you try to create a similar button within the YouTube annotations section you can't find that option anywhere! The trick is you don't create the button within YouTube but within your video editing software. This chapter is for advanced users because you will need to know how to graphic edit (Photoshop, Corel Draw, etc.) along with using your video editing software.

custom youtube buttons

The first thing you want to do is create the button within a graphic program such as Photoshop. The size of the image doesn't

matter as it will be resized within the video editing software. After you are done creating your image button, save the file as a jpeg or png image.

Next we need to boot up your video editing software. For this example I will be using Sony Vegas Pro.

custom youtube buttons

Be sure to import both your video file(s) and the button image. When placing the image on your timeline and layers, usually the image should be on the first layer so that it is on top of everything. You can see below I placed the

image on the first layer, resized and positioned the button to be in the top left of my video. Don't forget to stretch the button image for how long you want it to appear for. After this has been done, go ahead and render your video to be uploaded to YouTube.

custom youtube buttons

Once you have uploaded your video onto YouTube, go into the video manager section then edit your video. From here go into the annotations area for the video. In the 'Annotations' section, scroll to where you placed your image button in the timeline. You can do this with any of the annotation options YouTube has to offer. For my example I will be using the spotlight option. After adding the spotlight annotation, place it where your image button starts and stretch it to when it is gone. Edit your spotlight annotation options to have a border color which will stand out as a hyperlink for the button. You could also add some text below your spotlight if you feel your viewers might not understand it could be a button to click.

Now you need to check off the link option and set it to whichever option you would like. Whether it is another video, channel, subscribe, etc.

custom youtube buttons

The final steps is to add the URL of the link you wish the viewer to go to. Lastly at the top of the annotations page, select 'save' and 'publish' near the top of the settings. This will ensure your settings have been saved and your video is ready with the customized button(s).

When you play your video, you will see the image appears as a clickable button now.

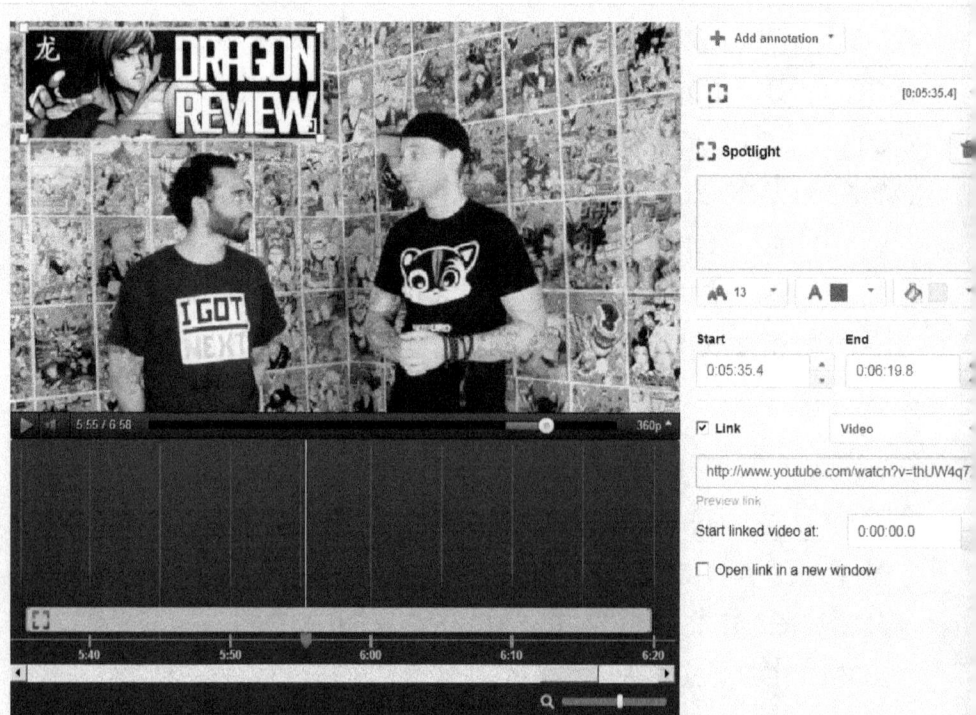

youtube ad information

Generally there are five different types of ads that viewers notice on YouTube. You can only view the ad details if you are a partner with YouTube or in contract with a YouTube network. To view the ad details and performance, log into your YouTube account and go to your video manager. Under the dashboard area click into the 'Analytics' section and within there is 'Earnings Reports'. Click on the 'Ad Performance' section.

PRIMARY AD TYPE	PLAYBACK-BASED CPM ↓	GROSS REVENUE	ESTIMATED MONETIZED PLAYBACKS
Auction TrueView In-stream	$12.68	$48.11	3,794
Standard Reserved In-stre...	$11.33	$3.20	283
Auction In-stream	$7.29	$0.47	65
Auction unknown	$5.52	$1.47	267
Auction display	$3.65	$24.65	6,749
Reserved display	$2.72	$0.35	129

1 - 6 of 6

youtube ad information

The first type of ad we will discuss is 'Auction TrueView In-stream' ads. These are the commercial ads which are inserted before or during a video. The viewers has the option to skip the ad.

'Standard Reserved In-stream' ads are the non-skippable ads which appear before, during and after videos. Usually these ads will generate the most profit and are sold on a reserve basis.

'Auction In-Stream' ads are also non-skippable ads that appear before, during and after videos. These are sold to advertisers via the adwords auction.

'Reserved Display' ads are rich media or images ads which appear as overlays on the video (usually the transparent text banners that disappear automatically) or as image ads on the watch page.

youtube ad information

'Auction Display' ads are rich media ads which appear as an image banner on the bottom of your videos or as a 300px by 250px image on the watch page. These ads are sold to advertisers via the adwords auction.

There are two ways advertisers place ads on YouTube:

1) Displaying ads on YouTube which are bid on and priced through the AdWords Auction.

2) Reserving a placement on the site through a YouTube sales representative or a DoubleClick media adviser. Normally called a 'Reserve Media Buy'.

You can find more details about YouTube ads on the Google support forum:
http://goo.gl/260WT

still under review

After uploading a video to YouTube and enabling monetization, Youtube may state that it cannot be monetized until it passes review. This bug, or 'terrible feature' as I'd like to call it, sometimes does not pass review for months or in some cases years! Thus preventing you from earning money from your video views.

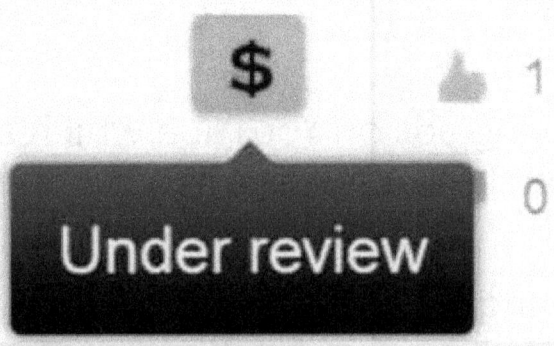

There are a few methods to get around this and most of them don't work. My method has worked for me almost 100% of the time. Before we start, you will need Google Chrome, Internet Explorer and Firefox.

still under review

Post your video using FireFox and then enable monetization. If the green $ icon expresses it's under review, try this first. Go back to your video manager page and play your video a few times. Then go back into the video manager to see if it turned on. *Sometimes* this works. If it doesn't, you will need to edit the video you just posted. Open notepad and copy and paste the video's title, description and keywords into notepad. Replace all fields with the word 'one' and save your videos. Now open Internet Explorer and log into your YouTube account. Navigate to the video and turn off monetization. Completely log out of YouTube in Internet Explorer. Then, using Google Chrome in incognito mode (CTRL + Shift + N), log into your YouTube account. Edit the video in question and enable monetization. Using Chrome, go to the video manager section and play your video. Hopefully you will now see a an advertisement within your video.

still under review

This will only work for newly posted videos. If your video has been waiting to be monetized for some time, you can try this trick but most likely you will need to delete the video and re-upload it.

I was told YouTube implemented this feature and it not a bug, but an effort by YouTube to prevent users from uploading material which is not owned by themselves and earning money. YouTube cannot verify every video on a daily basis to confirm if material has been stolen or not. This 'pausing' system gives YouTube more slack on controlling the cash flow which is awarded to users via Adsense.

fighting copyright strikes

I received my first copyright strike from Sony Japan. They made a claim against an anime video review that had no content, just myself talking. Crazy right? When your videos are claimed by other people, YouTube by law has to take your video down. This is very frustrating especially if that video is earning you high amounts of views and revenue. Since I am with several YouTube partners now, I do not get copyright strikes anymore. I can only provide the tools I used to fight back when I received them.

First you will either get an email from YouTube about the copyright complaint or you will notice a warning message appear in your YouTube account. Next, you will want to file a counter claim notification against whoever is trying to screw you. YouTube may ask you to watch their copyright school video and answer questions.

fighting copyright strikes

Go ahead and file a counter notification expressing that you are not breaking any laws per the fair use doctrine and any other details you deem necessary. I believe YouTube claims they will wait 14 days to review your case and possibly turn your video back on. YouTube WILL NOT turn your video on after 14 days. It took YouTube 2 months to turn back on my first video which was wrongly accused. Once it happened again, I did not want to wait 2 months for things to process, did some research and was able to get my video back online within 48 hours of the copyright claim.

After you submit your counter claim, you will need to fax YouTube. Emails will not work, they get tons of emails a day, but how many faxes do you think YouTube gets?

fighting copyright strikes

Don't worry if you have a fax machine or not. I used the website: www.GotFreeFax.com

You are able to send two free faxes a day with their service. Go to their site create an account and send a fax to YouTube.

YouTube's Fax number is: **1-650-872-8513**

Be sure to include all of the details from the Copyright Complaint email. After you do this, you should receive an email from YouTube within 24 hours and hopefully another 24hours later you video should be unblocked.

copyright@youtube.com

acknowledgments

The motivation I gained for writing this book came from the viewers of my YouTube channel(s). A big thanks goes to them. To my family which has supported me and all of my crazy ideas, including going to Japan. To my sister for letting me use her house as my studio for filming. To Jeff Max who has mentored me in proper business strategy and planning. To Carlos Arvelo who appeared several times on my YouTube show and never questioned my actions. Meeting with James & Arvin and having 'Law of Attraction' conversations. Jason Asher who pushed me to go forward with my show. Lastly, a big thanks to anyone else who I may have missed.

-Corey

to-do list

- Sign up for Google & YouTube
- Sign up for all Social Media outlets
- Sign up for Google Alerts
- Organize account details in a spreadsheet
- Download video editing software
- Download graphic editing software
- Create a show set or green screen
- Make sure your lighting is good
- Make sure your audio is perfect
- Update your channels profile with graphics, relevant keywords and a good description
- Practice recording yourself
- Practice video editing
- Upload a video & edit all values for the video
- Promote the video via social media
- Create a blog and post your videos there too
- Subscribe to Google Adsense
- Link YouTube with Adsense
- Enable monetization on all of your videos
- Make 1 video a week & promote, promote!!!

useful websites

Camtasia: http://www.techsmith.com/camtasia.html
Hootsuite: http://goo.gl/UCN3w
BH Photo: http://www.bhphotovideo.com/
Cowboy Studios: http://www.cowboystudio.com/
Social Blade: http://www.socialblade.com/
Fraps: http://www.fraps.com/
Google: http://www.google.com/
YouTube: http://www.youtube.com/
xSplit: http://www.xsplit.com/
Gimp: http://www.gimp.org
Jing: http://www.techsmith.com/jing.html
Audacity: http://audacity.sourceforge.net/
Photoshop: http://www.adobe.com
GotFreeFax: http://www.gotfreefax.com/

RuggedSource YouTube:
http://www.youtube.com/RuggedSource
SleepWalk Strategy YouTube:
http://www.youtube.com/SleepWalkStrategy

legal statement

The information contained in this program (including but not limited to any seminar content, manuals, CDs, recordings, mp3s, teleseminars or other content in any format) is based on sources and information reasonably believed to be accurate as of the time it was recorded or created. However, this material deals with topics that are constantly changing and are subject to ongoing changes RELATED TO TECHNOLOGY AND THE MARKET PLACE AS WELL AS LEGAL AND RELATED COMPLAINCE ISSUES. Therefore, the completeness and current accuracy of the materials cannot be guaranteed. These materials do not constitute legal, compliance, financial, tax, accounting, or related advice.

The end user of this information should therefore use the contents of this program and the materials as a general guideline and not as the ultimate source of current information and when appropriate the user should consult their own legal, accounting or other advisors.

Any case studies, examples, illustrations cannot guarantee that the user will achieve similar results. In fact, your results may vary significantly and factors such as your market, personal effort and many other circumstances may and will cause results to vary.

THE INFORMATION PROVIDED IN THIS PRODUCT IS SOLD AND PROVIDED ON AN "AS IS" BASIS WITH THE GUARANTEE BEING SIMPLY THAT IF YOU FOLLOW THE RECOMMENDATIONS PROVIDED AND DO NOT ACHIEVE THE STATED RESULTS, YOU CAN GET A REFUND. THOSE RESULTS ARE YOUR RESPONSIBILIY AS THE END USER OF THE PRODUCT. (SOME STATES DO NOT ALLOW LIMITED WARRANTIES, SO THIS MAY NOT APPLY TO YOU.) INPARTICULAR, SELLER SHALL NOT BE LIABLE TO USER OR ANY OTHER PARTY FOR ANY DAMAGES, OR COSTS, OF ANY CHARACTER INCLUDING BUT NOT LIMITED TO DIRECT OR INDIRECT, CONSEQUENTIAL, SPECIAL, INCIDENTAL, OR OTHER COSTS OR DAMAGES, IN EXCESS OF THE PURCHASE PRICE OF THE PRODUCT OR SERVICES. THESE LIMITATIONS MAY BE AFFECTED BY THE LAWS OF PARTICULAR STATES AND JURISDICTIONS AND AS SUCH MAY BE APPLIED IN A DIFFERENT MANNER TO A PARTICULAR USER.

This is just a legal statement to protect myself for those who buy my book and are too lazy to make good quality content for YouTube, then decide to possibly sue me for not generating money via Adsense or a network.

www.ingramcontent.com/pod-product-compliance
Lightning Source LLC
Chambersburg PA
CBHW060858170526
45158CB00001B/403